WORLD SOCIALISM
AT THE CROSSROADS

WORLD SOCIALISM *AT THE CROSSROADS*

An Insider's View

SILVIU BRUCAN

PRAEGER

New York
Westport, Connecticut
London

Library of Congress Cataloging-in-Publication Data

Brucan, Silviu, 1916-

World socialism at the crossroads.
Includes index.
1. Communism–History. 2. Communism and technology.
3. Communist countries–Economic policy. I. Title.
HX36.B76 1987 335.43'09 87-11704
ISBN 0-275-92782-2 (alk. paper)

Library of Congress Catalog Card Number: 87-11704
ISBN: 0-275-92782-2

First published in 1987

Praeger Publishers, One Madison Avenue, New York, NY 10010
A division of Greenwood Press, Inc.

Printed in the United States of America

The paper used in this book complies with the Permanent Paper Standard issued by the National Information Standards Organization (Z39.48-1984).

10 9 8 7 6 5 4 3 2 1

CONTENTS

PREFACE

This book was prompted by the prospect I envision that unless the socialist societies of the East adapt their system to the scientific-technological revolution (at least to the extent that the West already has), socialism will remain caught in the twentieth century, however paradoxical this may sound for a political philosophy designed for the future.

The idea throughout this book is that the scientific-technological revolution has touched the basics of society and all spheres of man's life much more deeply than the social and national revolutions of our time. Acknowledging this fundamental fact–unforeseen by Karl Marx–and drawing the proper conclusions is the major condition for maintaining Marxism's relevance at the end of this century and for reviving its analytical and predictive force. Therefore, the paramount task in the East today is to eliminate the obnoxious legacy of Stalinism and to liberate social theory from the shackles that have kept it stagnant for fifty years. This has had a devastating effect on all of the social sciences.

As we approach the new millenium, in which information and knowledge will dominate society's development, let us recall that the intellectual repression undertaken by the Inquisition in Italy and Spain–where the Renaissance and major breakthroughs in science had originated–caused the locus of scientific research and thought to shift to northern Europe and England.

My basic theoretical point is that although change will have to start from the *economic end*, it must necessarily involve social relations, and ultimately the political system and the Communist party itself. For only systemic change will allow the USSR to come to terms with the new stage of the scientific-technological revolution: computers, information technologies, and global communication. There is now sufficient evidence that Mikhail Gorbachev is aware of this.

But, while an overall and coherent scheme to reform Soviet society is shaping up in the Kremlin, new thinking in foreign policy is virtually limited by its status of superpower with global commitments and strategic objectives very much on the mind of the Soviet leadership. The fact is that neither the formulation of foreign policy nor the external behavior of the USSR originate in its domestic system alone. The international environment, particularly the interstate system, with its competitive dynamics and power game, has played an important role in shaping Soviet policy in world affairs. Therefore, changing Soviet society is not enough. For a really new Soviet foreign policy to emerge, the international interstate system must also undergo change.

In my 1983 book *The Post-Brezhnev Era* I noted that, "The passing of Brezhnev marked the end of an era in Soviet history," and that "the logic of politics will compel the successor of Brezhnev to provide an alternative to the stagnant society, sluggish economy, and placid foreign policy that have characterized the state of the USSR in recent years." My conclusion was: "The new Soviet leadership stands directly at the intersection of two eras, with one leg in the past and another about to step into the future. The dilemma it faces is formidable. One thing is clear: the men of the rising generation are neither emotionally attached nor politically committed to Stalin's legacy. They belong to the present day Soviet Union, a modern industrial country with an educated working class and a multi-million detachment of scientists, engineers, and trained managers; such a society cannot be run the same way as post-revolutionary peasant Russia. Here is the crux of the matter."

Four years later, this anticipation is coming true.

INTRODUCTION

World socialism is at the crossroads: Stronger than ever in the politico-military sphere, it is struggling with relative underdevelopment in the world market, a struggle that threatens its very existence as a new socio-economic system. While visiting the United States and some West European countries in 1985 and 1986, I was struck by the revelation that the economic technological gap dividing East from West is now wider than it was thirty years ago when I was Romania's ambassador to Washington. This disproves the basic premise upon which we in the East have been working to build a new and superior society designed eventually to replace capitalism.

Something must be wrong, either with the theoretical premise of socialism or with the way it was implemented. To discover the answer I critically examined the history of "real socialism": its nebulous past, its present crisis, and its potential for the future. It is my conviction as an East European writer that only Marx's analytical method can help disentangle what his professed followers in the East have so effectively entangled, partly because some of the initial assumptions were either wrong or chimeric.

Let me say at the outset that it is not the purpose of this critical examination to demonstrate that had Marx's teachings been implemented correctly everything would be fine in the East today. Rather, my purpose is to reveal the tension that developed from the beginning in Soviet Russia between theory and social reality and to study the domestic and international conditions that have shaped "real socialism" as it exists today. In fact, I maintain that the proper adjustment of theoretical premises to the new world and its social developments may well result in a vision of society somewhat different from that anticipated more than a century ago.

Marx was very clever when he refused to detail the specific features of communist society. Indeed, how could he anticipate that so many decades after the 1917 October Revolution the basic issue confronting socialist states would be to use or not to use the market to overcome a stagnant economy and technology that is laggard by present standards?

Yet, to a dialectical mind this question should not come as a surprise. I will argue that industrialization, whether under capitalism or socialism, cannot succeed without the impetus to the economy provided by market forces. In general, dialectics warns us against a purely linear and integral view of history as a cumulative chronology in which one social formation (e.g., feudalism or capitalism) supersedes another, only to produce eventually its own successor. In fact, capitalism's history has revealed the remanent force of the feudal legacy, and we have witnessed a strong comeback of the feudal spell even in socialist societies. And if socialism has borrowed so much from feudalism for its political system, why not borrow a device such as the market from capitalism to perform a function that is capitalist anyway!

1. The well-known historical condition that the socialist revolution started in less-developed countries compelled the post-revolutionary regimes to industrialize in order to catch up economically and technologically with capitalism. As long as the competition was over the degree of industrialization, everything worked according to plan: The socialist countries, less developed but enjoying a higher rate of growth, were slowly but surely catching up with the highly industrialized capitalist nations.

The scientific-technological revolution spoiled all that. In the West the new technologies were applied on a large scale, leading to a tremendous expansion of productive forces. In the East, precisely at the time when the task was set by the Communist party "to fuse the discoveries of the scientific-technological revolution with the advantages of the socialist economic system," a sharp drop in the rates of growth occurred—a 10 percent rate of growth in 1960 dropped to a recent low of 3 percent. The reason must be stated clearly and bluntly: The command-type planning system initiated by Stalin does not and cannot assimilate the scientific-technological revolution. Every small technological advance requires strenuous extra-economic efforts by party and state organs and an immense waste of resources. The spectacular Soviet achievements in outer space and modern weaponry have had no spill-over in the civilian industrial process precisely because of the unresponsiveness of the economic system to the new developments.

We in the East must have the courage to admit that our assessment of the relative behavior of the two competing systems once they faced the scientific-technological revolution has been proven wrong. The capitalists in the West have shown greater flexibility in innovating the productive process and greater mobility in adapting to rapid technological change. In the USSR, an economic system tailored when Russia was a backward peasant country has been stubbornly preserved for five decades; even the modest reforms initiated by Khrushchev and Kosygin to relax the heavy-handed planning system a bit were rescinded by party bureaucrats, who consolidated their control over the economy in the Brezhnev era.

Consequently, Western capitalism has been the main beneficiary of the technological revolution and is the winner of the latest round in the East-West competition. Between 1955 and 1980 the absolute gap between Eastern and Western per capita gross national product (GNP) almost doubled, increasing from $4,000 to $7,730. The share in world industrial production held by CMEA (Council for Mutual Economic Assistance, Comecon)–which had risen 10.6 points between 1950 and 1960, reaching 28.4 percent of the total–rose only 3.6 points between 1960 and 1970 and a mere 1 point between 1970 and 1982.

The talk in the East about the general crisis of capitalism has been deceptive. Dating the beginning of that crisis to the 1917 October Revolution may have been ideologically rewarding but has no scientific basis. The territorial expansion of socialist revolutions did not prevent capitalism from developing its productive forces and growing in per capita terms from 1950 to 1973 at a rate twice those of its most prosperous earlier periods. We should recall Marx's thesis: "No social order disappears before all the productive forces for which there is room in it have been developed and new higher relations of production never appear before the material conditions of their existence have matured in the womb of the old society."[1]

I submit that the life span of capitalism should be rather related to the industrial system; experience shows that within that system capitalism can develop its productive forces without serious restrictions. The demise of capitalism will occur when the new revolutionary technologies no longer find room within the limits of the industrial system based on machines, electric power, and material productive forces. The current inability of Western economies to absorb the tens of millions of unemployed even at a time of economic upturn is the first signal of such restrictions taking shape.

2. I will argue that the turnabout caused by the revolution in science and technology requires a reexamination of socialist economic policy—past, present, and future—from an entirely new perspective. In fact, the whole Marxist-Leninist approach to the building of a communist society must be thoroughly revised: It is outdated and therefore lacks a clear vision of the future.

Let me start by noting that from a Marxist viewpoint such notions as socialist society, socialist state, and socialist economic system have no ground on which to stand. Marx spoke of only two types of society, each with a different mode of production: capitalist and communist. It was Stalin who invented the notion of "socialist society" as an intermediate form between capitalist and communist, thus introducing in an ongoing process of change a sort of halting point at which the process must presumably stop and pause. And here is the trick, because once such a notion is accepted, the socialist society becomes an end in itself, something that must be strengthened, defended, and of course preserved by all means. The cause of revolution is at stake! In other words, we are faced with an established order, the ideology of which necessarily acquires a status quo orientation.

The issue has since become highly controversial. Some authors speak instead of "state capitalism"[2]; others feel that it is neither capitalist nor socialist but a society with its own mode of production, labeling it "collectivist" or "etatist".[3] My opinion is that we are dealing with a combination of elements typical of a transition period in which the old capitalist relations have not been totally eliminated while the new socialist relations are still in the making. Because private ownership of the means of production has been abolished, the state becoming their owner and manager, I call this system *state socialism* with the proviso that it is more state than socialism.

As for the economic system, since it represents merely the first phase of a communist society that has no base of its own, Stalin's economic model is chiefly a political ideological construct in which social (the ruling class or group) and political (monopoly of power at the top) considerations prevail over economic ones, forcing the economy to function according to those vested social and political interests. The coexistence within the economy of contradictory elements is not settled peacefully by economic means; it is political power that tries to overcome conflicting economic laws and tendencies by administrative means. Hence, political organs become an integral part of the economic process; they prime the economy every day and every hour to make it function. Clearly such a heavy-handed system is organically hostile to a scientific-technological revolution that threatens not only its viability but also the power structure so deeply entrenched in it.

Therefore, the proposal for economic reform is designed first and foremost to reinstate the primacy of economic criteria in the organization and function of the socialist economy, with the final aim of setting up an economic system that would function on the basis of its own motive forces and logic—that is, function as a self-regulating mechanism. Of course, to do that the economic laws and categories that apply in the transition period must first be considered. This is precisely what Lenin had in mind with his NEP (New Economic Policy). I feel that in an underdeveloped country that did not go through a capitalist stage of development, Lenin's NEP is a strategy of development for *the entire period of industrialization.*

3. The next point I will make is that not only socialist society but also future communist society are conceived in the East within the limits of an industrial system that belongs to the capitalist epoch. It all started when Stalin presented industrialization as the goal of socialism. Actually, industrialization is a big capitalist operation; bourgeois economists formulated the theory of industrialization and capitalists have invented the ways and means to carry it out. The Bolshevik party had no choice but to follow those teachings and practices by resorting to capital accumulation and all that goes with it in order to get the surplus for industrial investments. The only issue that troubled the communist leaders was whether to accumulate at the expense of the peasant sector, or of the urban population, and the relative proportion of each. This problem continues to this day in all socialist countries, and in this context a return to Lenin's NEP with its emphasis on the market appears to be a sensible proposition. In other words, industrialization should be at best the premise of a socialist society but not its goal.

The international environment reinforces this argument in the sense that we operate in a world economic system based on the predominance of industry; the economic system is influenced by the industrial structures of dominance built into the system by Western capitalism. Hence, the assumption that a socialist nation consolidates its independent socialist stance by industrializing is a delusion. In fact, the more industrialized a country, the deeper it gets involved in a world economy that is becoming more interdependent and compact due to the organizational force of the technological revolution. Industrialization probably is the greatest factor in integrating the world economy; it makes nations more dependent on fluctuations in technology and prices on the world market, as we in the East have noticed lately with sorrow.

By placing socialism within the historical and conceptual context of the capitalist industrial epoch, the Soviet Union's prospective view of communist society has been adapted to that epoch. Lenin's goal of total electrification and Stalin's definition of the threshold to communism in terms of millions of tons of pig iron, steel, coal, and oil (which, by the way, have long been attained in the USSR) serve only to indicate the limitation of their historical perspective within the industrial system. At a time when in most advanced countries the smokestack industries are losing ground and society is stepping into the era of computers, information, and telecommunication, the Soviets will have to surpass the industrial system in order to advance toward communism. Today, communism should be viewed as a *post-industrial society*.

4. My conclusion in Chapter 2 is that not only the economic system but the political system is outdated. A system that keeps under strict control typing and photocopying machines as well as all other kinds of information can hardly come to terms with computers, information, and communication technologies. To democratize and modernize such a system, one must strike at the very core of its power structure. Following are the essential changes I consider necessary to that end:

A. Because of historical circumstances and political tradition, including the socialist tradition, the appropriate form for a democratic and fairly representative political system in the East is *party pluralism*, rather than a multi-party system. To acquire political legitimacy for the one-party system, the Communist party must include representatives of all classes and major social groups which exist in socialist society and must guarantee them every opportunity to defend their specific interests and express their views. Otherwise, the emergence of alternative political parties is inevitable and legitimate.

The acceptance of groups and factions within the party is the fundamental principle of party democracy. I will document historically that ever since factions have been forbidden, the result has been that one faction (Stalin's, Khrushchev's, or Brezhnev's) has invariably run the party by eliminating the others. Here lies the origin of the intolerant and repressive nature of the Communist party, the rule that suffocates the normal political and ideological life of the party.

The legalization of factions should start with the publication and critical examination of the works of Stalin, Bukharin, and Trotsky, without which the Revolution and the Bolshevik party itself are denied their history.

B. The power of decision making in the Communist party must be restored to its elected supreme organs—the Congress and the Central Committee, as provided in the Party Rules (Statute).

Stalin's improper stratagem to remove the center of decision making from elected and deliberative bodies to the top hierarchical organs of the bureaucracy—the Politburo and the Secretariat—has led to the bureaucratization of the Communist party; the Congress and the Central Committee have been reduced to rubber-stamp bodies that are convened merely to endorse decisions already made in secret by the Politburo and Secretariat.

C. The system of virtual life-peerage enjoyed by party leaders, regardless of their political performance, must be abolished. It has been the source of power abuse, personality cult, nepotism, above-the-law behavior, and corruption.

Members of the Central Committee may be elected by Congress for a maximum of four terms (sixteen years) and members of the Politburo and Secretariat for a maximum of two terms (eight years). The latter cannot hold positions in the executive branch of government.

D. The principle of separation of powers among the executive, legislative, and judiciary branches of government will be introduced and strictly observed. To that end, an election system will be elaborated, providing for the nomination of candidates by local citizens without interference from the central party organs. For

> every official function, a minimum of two candidates will be nominated.
>
> In general, the working class (now predominant numerically, better educated, and more experienced politically) is no longer willing to accept the situation in which a small and privileged group exercises power on its behalf. The time has come for socialist democracy to be installed through the *direct* participation of the working class in both economic management and political governance.

With the coming to power in Moscow of the new generation of political leaders, the question of change in the East is on the agenda. In chapter 3 we will explore the stimuli for and restrictions to change in the East today, both domestic and international, as well as the intricate question of whether and how such change is possible given the well-entrenched and petrified political structure of power.

The new Program of the Soviet Communist Party (1986) and Mikhail Gorbachev's statements are permeated with the recognition of a need for change in Soviet society, for "a radical renewal of its material and technical foundation on the basis of the scientific-technological revolution," and for "promoting socialist self-government by the people." Gorbachev spoke of the need for "basic change in the economy and in the whole system of social relations."

However, the official rhetoric appears more radical than the practical measures suggested by the party Congress. There is an obvious disproportion between the magnitude of the problem, attributed to Brezhnev's failure to grasp the importance of the scientific-technological revolution, and the modest reforms announced to deal with that problem. Although the key word of the program is "acceleration" to regain lost ground, Gorbachev seems to move very cautiously when it comes to the structural pillars of the old system. And he is probably right to do so, for the radical reform he mentioned in his final aim not only would have to break the resistance of the party bureaucrats but also would have to overcome the reluctance of many managers to embark on an independent course that implies risk. Above all, he would have to face the deep-seated idea of workers that they should enjoy job security, equal pay, and bonuses, regardless of their work performance.

Having dealt with domestic conditions myself, I anticipate that the degree and speed of change in the Soviet system will be determined chiefly by strategic considerations. The strategic position of the CMEA in the world economy is defined by three percentages: roughly 32 percent of all world industrial production, but only 11 percent of world trade and merely 9 percent of world financial transactions. This reveals a low competitiveness in industrial products and a limited capability to influence processes on the world market.

The truly crucial development that seems to have alarmed the new Soviet leadership, however, is the advent of the so-called "third industrial revolution" involving the computerization of economic and social activities and the large-scale introduction of microelectronics and robots in the industrial process. Here the prospect of a serious technological lag vis-à-vis advances in the West has become apparent. Nothing looks more convincing in this respect than the position of the USSR and its partners in the high tech contest now raging on the world markets: They simply do not count in that race. The critical question confronting the East is, how long can socialist economies survive as such while the capitalist core becomes more and more computerized and informational? This is not only an economic issue, for at the end of this century there can be no strong ideological influence from a second-rate technological base.

5. Finally, in this book I review the vacillations in Soviet strategic concepts throughout the history of the socialist world and I perceive the emergence of an alternative strategy originating in China.

From the beginning the USSR had to struggle for the two major strategic objectives of its leadership: the fundamental economic task of catching up with capitalism and the politico-military aim of acquiring a world posture sufficiently strong to withstand the challenges from the hostile capitalist environment. After the collapse of détente, the choice of strategy tilted in favor of the latter, and eventually the USSR succeeded in building a politico-military force that allows it to display initiative on the world scene affecting, for better or for worse, the international political climate. Surely the Soviets could do nothing of that sort in the world economy, where their actions are adaptive rather than disruptive.

The issue of strategy is pushed on the agenda by a sober appraisal of the state of affairs in all three subsystems of our world: (1) the socialist countries are losing in their economic-technological competition with the West; (2) in the West, at a time when the capitalist economy is going through a protracted crisis with high unemployment, the communist parties are losing ground; (3) in the Third World, Marxist-Leninist regimes are wrestling with difficult economic problems while a series of countries in the Pacific following the capitalist road enjoy high rates of economic growth.

World politics as a whole require a review of strategy, for in the nuclear era the use of force has ceased to be the decisive factor in changing power relations. Global geopolitics is being increasingly reshaped by economic and technological assets rather than by traditional military means.

Currently the strongest contenders in the economic contest are the United States, with its formidable financial power, and Japan, whose exports are nearly double those of the Soviet Union and whose gross national product is close to surpassing that of the USSR. But a different type of challenge is coming from the other end of the spectrum—China. The leadership of China is probably the first to have grasped the new reality of geopolitics, making the boldest turnabout in modern history: from military buildup to an economic drive for modernization. Were its billion people to become a modern productive force, the world power constellation would be radically changed.

Projections to the year 2010 calculated on the basis of recent trends in GNP growth indicate that the Soviet Union faces the prospect of being pushed back from second to fourth place in the world economy, behind the United States, China, and Japan.

A tragic reappraisal now is due in Moscow. The main lesson of seven decades of socialist experience is that politico-military advances resulting from certain favorable conditions in the class struggle cannot long be maintained unless an adequate economic infrastructure is built to support them. Failure to do this will allow the dynamic forces of capitalism to roll back the political advances of socialism, as we now see happening on the world scene. It is this mechanism of the world system that explains the tendencies of some socialist countries to resist those pressures through militarization and repressive internal policies.

In this context, China is emerging as the champion of an alternative socialist strategy based primarily on economic success and popular well-being. Such a strategy proceeds from the recognition that the territorial expansion of socialism has reached a point where it must stop for a while and consolidate its positions by building an economic system sufficiently modern and competitive to withstand the challenges from the capitalist core. This is the gist of Deng Xiao Ping's principle of "one state, two systems," suggesting that while continental China will modernize its socialist economy, Hong Kong and Taiwan will retain their capitalist system for 50 years or so; yet all will belong to one state–China. If the urban reform produces the same result as the rural reform, the new strategy is bound to acquire a tremendous following, particularly in the Third World. The Kremlin is thus confronted with a dramatic choice: to cling to the old ways and rely increasingly on military power as its main asset, or to take the bull by the horns and proceed with a radical change in both economic policy and global strategy. The issue of leadership in the communist movement is virtually at stake in that choice. In fact, the future of the world may depend on that choice.

Notes

1. Lewis Feuer, ed.*Marx and Engels*, (New York: Doubleday Anchor, 1959), p. 44.

2. Actually, Lenin starting talking about state capitalism in April or May 1918, trying to emphasize the concessions that had to be made to the existing capitalist structure and control of the economy. After the period of "war communism," when the Bolshevik party jumped to the other extreme, abolishing whatever capitalism remained in the economy, Lenin returned to state capitalism, identifying it with the NEP. Many authors consider Stalinism and state capitalism to be equivalent. Tony Cliff, in *Russia: A Marxist Analysis* (London, 1964), argues that the Stalinist bureaucracy is a class and that the society is capitalist, although in a modified version due to the absence of private ownership of the means of production. Trying hard to substantiate his theory of state capitalism with quotations from Marx, Engels, Lenin, and Bukharin, Cliff maintains that state capitalism is a transitional form that was practically impossible before the Revolution but became possible after the Revolution had nationalized ownership and had to cope with the task of capital accumulation. His conclusion: A social, not just a political, revolution (here he differs with Trotsky) is required to overthrow the state capitalist order.

The theme of state capitalism has been rather popular in Yugoslav literature. Even before the war, Anton Pannekoek characterized the

Soviet system as state capitalism and its state bureaucracy as a new ruling class in *Lenin as Philosopher* (Belgrade, 1938), which shows that Milovan Djilas's theory of the "new class" had roots in his own country's earlier social thought. Branko Horvat himself admits that he was attracted in the late 1960s by the notion of state capitalism in *An Essay on Yugoslav Society* (White Plains, N.Y., 1969).

As for official Soviet doctrine, Lenin's notion of state capitalism has been totally forgotten. A. T. Lepeskhin divides the history of socialist society into three stages: (1) the dictatorship of the proletariat, which is the period of change from capitalism to socialism; (2) the period of gradual transfer of the dictatorship to an all-people's state, during which all the conditions for the full-scale formation of communism are prepared; and (3) the period of the all-people's state, which develops after the full and final victory of socialism (*Obshchenarodnoe gosudarstvo i ego osnovnye cherty*, Moscow: GIP, 1961, no. 3, p. 22). Recently in contrast to Khrushchev's emphasis that the state of the entire people represented a "most important milestone" in the evolution of socialist statehood, Soviet theorists have challenged those who present the situation "as though our state had already lost its class nature, had ceased to be a class state, and was losing even the character of political power. But that of course is clearly running ahead and is very harmful both theoretically and practically....The state does not cease to have a class character as a whole, nor is it deprived of class content," writes V. M. Chkhikvadze (*Razvitie narodnoi sushchnosti sotsialisticheskogo gosudarstva*, Moscow: GIP, 1966, no. 10, p. 8). Finally, an authoritative theorist, D. Chesnokov, speaks of the continued growth of the economic-organizational and cultural-educational functions of the socialist state during the period of communist construction (*Nekotorye aktual'nye voprosy markisto-leniniskoi teorii*, Moscow, 1967).

3. Max Schachtman, an American Marxist, has this to say: "This new social order...is neither capitalist nor proletarian. To distinguish it from either one of these two and at the same time to underline its outstanding characteristics as tersely as possible, this new state was designated as bureaucratic collectivism" (*The Bureaucratic Revolution*, New York: Donald Press, 1962, p. 62). The Italian author Bruno Rizzi was one of the first to take this view (*La bureaucratisation du monde*, Paris, 1939), and now quite a few Italian leftists have adopted this notion.

Branko Horvat of Yugoslavia prefers the term etatism defined thusly: "A society will be called etatist if its ruling strata profess the basic tenets of traditional socialist ideology, such as the elimination of private productive property and the emancipation of the exploited classes, but revise the socialist approach in regard to one crucially important aspect: the role of the state" (*The Political Economy of Socialism*, Armonk, N.R.: Sharpe, 1982). However, bureaucratic collectivism as opposed to bureaucratic individualism (presumably capitalist society) does not cover the nature of the relationship of production, the very feature I consider essential in the definition of a society; nor does etatism speak about that relationship–it could be applied equally to capitalist society at a time when the capitalist state plays an increasing role in the management of the economy and society. Horvat argues against the notion of state capitalism on the ground that it implies the existence of capitalists whom it is difficult to identify in etatist societies (p. 47); he also objects to state socialism as the initial phase of socialist development "because (1) state ownership is not a transitional stage between capitalism and socialism; (2) complete state monopoly of economic and political power is not a precondition for transition; (3) if state socialism is a transitional period, it will be short, with a clear tendency present for the role of the state to be reduced to its proper dimensions and for typically socialist institutions to be developed. In contemporary etatist societies, this is not the case" (p. 47). Here, again, the whole demonstration underestimates the nature of the relationship of production as a basic element in defining society. Furthermore, the assumption is that we are dealing with a developed capitalist society that is perfectly ripe for a normal transition to socialism and ultimately communism and, therefore, to which we can apply the classical Marxist paradigm in the analysis of the transition period.

I submit that under the particular historical condition of the Russian Revolution, state ownership was a must for the simple reason that socialist ownership presupposes the existence of a proletariat sufficiently numerous and educated to take over the ownership and management of the means of production. This indeed was not the case in post-revolutionary Russia. As for Horvat's third objection–that state socialism should be short (which implies its acceptance as a "necessary transitional stage")–I agree that this is desirable practically and necessary theoretically in order to reconstruct the Marxist paradigm. However, the trouble is that this is a real world, and in the real world we are faced with the dynamics of power, a phenomenon that the concept of the transition from capitalism to communism as a linear, one-directional process simply does not take into account. Once state socialism was instituted and a bureaucratic structure came into being to prop it up, an organic propensity developed in the bureaucracy to resist further change and to perpetuate itself in power. My point is that this is not sufficient reason to deny a society the merit of having abolished private property as a means of production and the extraction of surplus value by private capitalists that goes with it. Surely, the coming to power of fascism in Germany and Italy was not sufficient reason for Marxists to hesitate calling the respective societies capitalist, as long as the private ownership of the means of production and the profit motive remained in place. For a Marxist, the nature of the political superstructure is not the essential feature in the definition of a social formation.

Finally, let me deal with Horvat's conclusion: "What might have been a transitional, state socialist, period crystalized into a well established system that shows no tendency toward basic structural changes" (p. 47). Although I agree with the first part of that statement, I strongly disagree with the latter part. Every social system is inherently opposed to structural change; it is the economic and social contradictions within the system that ultimately bring about such change. I see no reason why one should consider that in the East European system such contradictions do not exist—hence, that their final outcome will not result in structural changes. The process may take a long time, but my opinion is that it has already begun, and this is what this book is all about.

1

THE PAST

RIGHT TIME, WRONG PLACE

Most historians will agree that World War I created propitious internal conditions for the social upheaval and political crisis in Russia that culminated in the 1917 October Revolution. The successive defeats suffered by the Russian army on the front combined with the economic chaos in the country. The shortage of fuel and the dislocation of the transportation system resulted in a drastic cut of industrial production; agricultural output dropped considerably, generating a food crisis —all having devastating effects on the currency of the country. The protracted war and the economic chaos caused extreme discontent among the working people; in the cities the workers began to strike and demonstrate against the government while in the countryside the peasants were losing hope of ever receiving land and peace from the Czar and his bourgeois allies. On the front, information about the disastrous conditions at home reached the soldiers; they refused to go into action against the enemy, voluntarily surrendered or inflicted wounds upon themselves, and deserted in masses. The Bolshevik party and other revolutionary forces organized the insurrection according to Lenin's plan and successfully carried out the Revolution.

Externally, conditions were equally propitious. The clash between the Triple Entente and the Austro-German alliance was so sharp and absorbing that Lenin could cite it as a factor that made the success of the Russian Revolution possible. The contest for world power positions dominated international affairs, pushing class-ideological considerations to the background. Only later, when Western chancelleries took notice of the revolutionary character of Russian developments, was the intervention of fourteen states initiated to quell the revolution. But the Soviet regime was already well established.

However, Russia in 1917, by general consent, was not ripe for a socialist transformation from the viewpoint of what is usually called objective conditions. Marx's view of society as a postcapitalist formation could hardly fit the Russian reality, either economically (the few industrial plants were just beginning to develop and agriculture was archaic) or socially (the country was predominantly peasant and the proletarian core had virtually melted away). Lenin had stated time and again that a socialist revolution in backward Russia could never succeed: He spoke of a larger revolution in Europe, beginning in Germany, that would carry Russia with it. Even Stalin, up to 1924, had this to say: "To overthrow the bourgeoisie the efforts of a single country suffice; the history of our own revolution attests to this. For the definite victory of socialism, for the organization of socialist production, the efforts of a single country are no longer sufficient; the efforts of the proletarians of several advanced countries are required."[1] Indeed, as long as Western capitalism is predominant in the world economic system—thus compelling all countries, regardless of their inner structures, to follow its commercial and financial rules on the world market—socialism cannot assert itself in one country or in several less-developed countries as a superior form of social organization.

In brief, historical conditions were such that reality in the USSR was in sharp contrast to the promised society. Two ways of dealing with that sensitive issue were available to the Bolshevik leaders: to admit candidly that socialism was far away and to tell the people they would have to work hard for a very long time to advance on that path, beginning with bourgeois democratic reforms and—what appears today even more important—an economic policy designed to catch up and eventually surpass capitalist performances; or to gloss over the gap between socialism and reality and to adjust the socialist model to the conditions of underdevelopment.

As usually happens in politics, the Bolshevik leaders used both ways and eventually Stalin settled for the second option. Lenin had emphasized the backwardness of Russia in such blunt language that most of his statements in this respect had to be later forgotten. Stalin continued to do the same for a while, until he switched in 1924 to the slogan "Socialism in one country." Only twelve years later, Stalin hastily proclaimed the USSR a socialist state and endowed it with the 1936 constitution claiming to mark the USSR's attainment of socialism.[2] From then on, that became the official ideological outlook.

Reality, however, was very different. To be sure, the global industrial output of the USSR in 1936 was the world's second, after that of the United States, but in productivity and per capita output the USSR was lagging behind all industrial countries. Labor productivity, which Lenin considered essential in the competition with capitalism, was four or five times lower than that in advanced countries. In agriculture, the performance was even poorer: grain output barely surpassed that under czarism (96 million tons in 1936 compared to 80 million tons in the years 1913 to 1916), and production of cattle, pigs, and sheep was much lower than that before the Revolution. If we take into account also that agriculture had to feed an urban population three times more numerous than that before the Revolution, we may easily understand why the Soviet people suffered from a chronic food shortage.

As for the socialist democracy and the guarantee of rights and freedoms proclaimed in the constitution, we must remember that those were the years of Gulag, mass repression, and terror directed not so much against the class enemy as against the class brothers, including Communist leaders and activists.

Of the 139 members and candidates of the party's Central Committee who had been elected at the seventeenth Congress, 98 persons (70 percent) were arrested and shot, mostly in 1937-38, right after the constitution was adopted. That was the state of reality.

I want to point out here that we are not dealing only with a striking incongruence between ideological image and the state of reality. Important also is that the notion of socialist society was conceived by Stalin in opposition to Marx's theory (faithfully adopted by Lenin in *State and Revolution*) concerning the transition period between capitalism and communism—a period of revolutionary transformation in which no stopover had been envisioned in the classics of historical materialism. Such theoretical constructs as socialist society or socialist republic represent an attempt to introduce to an ongoing process of change a pause during which the process must presumably stop for consolidation. And here is the trick, because once such a notion is accepted, the socialist society, particularly the socialist state, becomes an end in itself, something that must be strengthened, defended, and of course preserved by all means. The cause of the revolution is at stake! In other words, we are faced with another established order, the ideology of which necessarily acquires a status quo orientation.

Briefly, socialist society is the non-Marxist concept that has been inserted into socialist ideology by Stalin with the view of strengthening the regime over which he was presiding. That concept has become the core of conservatism that permeates Soviet ideology; in practice it has been used throughout Eastern Europe to halt the process of change toward communism.*

---

*For the sake of theoretical clarity, socialism (or socialist nations, states, etc.) will be used henceforth in Marxist terms, as the first phase of communist society.

Indeed, Marx spoke of only two types of society, each based on its own very different mode of production: capitalist and communist. "Between capitalist and communist society," he emphasized, "lies the period of the revolutionary transformation of the former into the latter."[3] True, he mentioned a first phase of Communist society as distinct from its higher phase, but he pointed out that this "is not a communist society which has developed on its own foundation, but on the contrary one which is just emerging from capitalist society, and which therefore in all respects–economic, moral and intellectual–still bears the birthmarks of the old society from whose womb it sprung."[4] Although seventy years in the USSR and forty years in Eastern Europe have elapsed since their revolutions, Marx's definition of the first phase is a fair description of those societies as they are today.

It is revealing that for the last decade or so not a single official document in the USSR or Eastern Europe, not a single learned journal, has dealt with the problems implicit in the higher stage of a Communist society. This is surely abnormal in a society that is presumably future-oriented, a society that is supposed to march toward communism. Rather, every theoretical effort is directed toward maintaining the established order, whether it is called real socialism or developed socialism.

This contradictory evolution (which is quite natural in a dialectical perspective of historical development) raises the important theoretical question of whether Marx's paradigm of the long period of transition from capitalism to communism did not underestimate or ignore altogether the very dynamics of political power. Indeed, historical experience tells us that political power is inherently opposed to a continuous flow of social change over time; political power in a post-revolutionary society will always tend to consolidate itself through a state structure–a bureaucratic structure, to be sure –whose organic propensity is to resist further change and to struggle to perpetuate its power. This is what happened in various phases of the French Revolution (the Committee of Public Safety, the Thermidor,* the Directory, and the Napoleonic Empire). Because of this political propensity to resist change, we are faced with the most striking paradox in the history of social revolutions: The socialist state has become the single greatest barrier on the path of East European societies toward communism.

THE CAPITALIST ENVIRONMENT

What has been the impact of joining the international interstate system and integration into the world economic system on the behavior of socialist nations? This issue has been systematically dodged in the Marxist literature of the East for reasons we will explore soon.

The official claim is that the revolution has produced a state that behaves differently from capitalist states in international affairs, a claim that makes peace and socialism synonymous. Khrushchev spoke of "a new type of international relations" guiding socialist states. As for economic relations, the prevailing view until recent times was that socialist economies, due to their planning system, would continue their upward movement no matter what happened in the capitalist world economy. And yet, the first international act of the Soviet Union

*Actually, Marx saw in the Thermidor the tendency of a revolution to acquire a new form of statehood, thus becoming very quickly a conservative force, a repressive mechanism for its own social order. The state, every state, is thus seen as essentially a conservative force for the preservation of the status quo. His theoretical solution for the coming of communism was, therefore, the withering away of the state.

that baffled people everywhere was the Molotov-Ribbentrop Pact of 1939, which bound two sworn class enemies by a secret understanding that included, among other things, the partition of Poland. Others followed:

- After World War II, in the early 1960s, U.S. and Soviet experts, in secret meetings, drafted two nuclear treaties (test ban and nonproliferation) that were presented jointly by the United States and the USSR at the United Nations. The treaties were rejected by France and China on the grounds that they were designed to secure for the two superpowers a virtual duopoly of nuclear strategic weapons and of basic decisions on war and peace.
- The hard polemics that broke out between the USSR and China were soon followed by military hostilities on the Ussuri River and the most massive concentration of troops along the Sino-Soviet border. A central issue in the dispute between the two socialist powers was territorial claims.
- In 1968, Soviet troops and other Warsaw Pact units invaded Czechoslovakia to overthrow the duly elected leadership of the Communist party and government of that socialist country.
- Later, with Soviet help and backing, Vietnam invaded Cambodia to dislodge the Communist leadership and installed in Phnom Penh a pro-Vietnamese faction that is maintained in power by about 200,000 Vietnamese soldiers. Related to this, large-scale military operations occurred in 1979 between China and Vietnam; Chinese leaders stated that the war against the Vietnamese was meant "to teach them a lesson."
- In late 1979, the Soviet Union invaded Afghanistan while its leader was being murdered, and installed in Kabul a new president. Since then, about 100,000 Soviet soldiers have been engaged in military operations against local guerrilla movements.

These are undeniable facts, whatever the motivations or reasons that prompted each of these international actions involving socialist nations. What is their theoretical or ideological significance?

Ideologically, the official propaganda is based on two theories formulated by Stalin. In 1927, he emphasized that the October Revolution represented "a revolution with an international, world character, since it means a radical turning point in the universal history of mankind, the turning point between the old capitalist world and the new socialist world."[5] What is missing in Stalin's appraisal is precisely the *international interstate system* and its impact on the policy of states and on politico-military developments in the world arena. While it is true that the emergence of the first socialist state, the USSR, produced a breakthrough in the capitalist system that has been widened subsequently by the successful revolutions in Eastern Europe, China, and other continents, it is equally true that the *structure* of the interstate system based on nation-states has remained basically unaltered. And so have remained the patterns of behavior molded by nation-states according to differences among them in size, power, and wealth. This is why students of international relations find that the foreign policy and external behavior of socialist nations are invariably influenced by their size, power, and level of development. The USSR makes full use of its great power status, playing a major role in world affairs and in the solution of international problems on all continents. A number of socialist nations that are less developed or underdeveloped (e.g., China, Cuba, Vietnam and Romania) have joined the group of seventy-seven countries in the battle for a new international economic order, while Yugoslavia has become one of the founders of the nonaligned movement.

Lenin has warned that revolution in Russia or in less-developed countries would not be enough; only revolution "at least in several advanced countries" could make socialism "capable of exercising a decisive influence upon world politics as a whole."[6] However, the capitalist core, the West, has survived the revolutionary sweeps in the wake of World Wars I and II and is alive and kicking. Thus, the socialist nations have had to adjust to the pattern of behavior prevailing in the international interstate system. Up to now they have failed to display either the necessary strength or the political will to change the structure of that system. And as the saying goes, if you can't beat them, join them.

Stalin's second theory, that the world market would split into two world markets, one capitalist and the other socialist, has proven equally erroneous.[7] Witness the profound effects on the Soviet Union of oil price fluctuations in world markets. Poland, Romania, and Yugoslavia have been compelled to slow their investment policies and adopt belt-tightening measures in order to cope with high interest rates set by Western banks for debtor nations. Even economic relations among socialist nations are affected by the trends on the world market, as illustrated by the new oil price set by the Soviets after the OPEC decision in the mid-seventies. A Soviet joke has it: After world socialism, Switzerland should remain a capitalist reservation to set the world prices! In short, the world economy is a hierarchical system in which Western capitalism holds a commanding position that allows it to dictate the rules of the game on the world market. Socialist nations play a marginal role because of their limited economic and financial potential.

At the heart of Stalin's theoretical position lies the postulate still prevailing in Soviet literature that class interests constitute the decisive motive force not only in society but also in international politics; on that basis we are treated to a dichotomous image of a world made up of two rival camps, capitalism and socialism. There are, to be sure, theorists who still cling to such a reductionist description of world politics and care very little that an increasing number of events, processes, and phenomena such as those mentioned in this chapter can no longer be integrated in their conceptual framework, beginning with conflicts of interest between socialist states themselves. The basic reason the dynamics of nation-state relations differ from those of class relations can be found in the particular dynamics of the interstate system. For nations are great and small, mighty and weak, developed and underdeveloped, rich and poor, and such disparities and inequalities generate a type of conflict and cooperation utterly different from that triggered between classes by contradictions in the mode and social relations of production.[8]

The degree of integration into the world economic system experienced by the USSR and other socialist nations has varied over time. In 1917, when the Revolution broke out in Russia, the world economic system was loose enough to allow the Soviet state to take shape in defiance of a predominant capitalism; the new power then was able to seal its borders and concentrate on the internal front: "socialism in one country." Today, however, the world system is tightly interdependent. Such radical isolation and delinking is no longer possible, although even now the degree of economic and political relations between the socialist nations and the rest of the world may vary according to prevailing circumstances.

We may conclude that the amount of behavior conformity in the interstate system depends on the intensity of relations binding a nation-state to its international environment, to the world economy.

Here we must keep in mind the relative strength of socialist nations in economic versus politico-military relations. Built into the heart of the dominant structures of the world economic system is the so-called First World and its industrial civilization that allows Western capitalism to dictate the rules of the game in the world market. In the politico-military sphere, however, the USSR and its allies succeeded after World War II to build a force that allows the USSR to be autonomous and thus to display political and military initiative on the world scene.

This is why the interstate system and the world economic system, however intertwined and interactive, are not synonymous. In general, political relations among nations and the way they crystallize in the world power structure do not necessarily reflect or parallel international economic relations and the hierarchical organization of the world economy. As an example, China plays a major role in world politics, while economically it is in a preindustrial stage; its economic and financial capability on the world market is less than that of Taiwan.

Later we will see how political and economic relations affect Soviet and East European policies. For now, let me stress that neither the formulation of foreign policy nor the external behavior of the USSR, China, or other socialist nations can be explained in terms of their internal socioeconomic system, class structure, or ideology alone. It is, rather, the interstate system, with its political dynamics, its power game, and its national rivalries, and the capitalist world economic system, driven by its endless accumulation and the tendency of the rich and developed to exploit the poor and underdeveloped, that may help us understand the baffling and contradictory behaviors of the socialist nations.

Political relations between states as crystallized in the international interstate system have an impact upon the socialist nations that neither Marx nor Lenin anticipated. It is precisely the unforeseen role of the political factor at both the internal and international levels that has upset the simplistic linear view of a transition from capitalism to communism based on the development of economic and social factors alone. In fact, the international state system is both historically and logically the political superstructure of the capitalist world economy.[9] These two systems reinforce each other; we cannot deal with the latter without settling affairs with the former.

In a previous book I wrote of a coming revolution that may well be more painful, although not necessarily more violent, than its predecessors; for it will deal not only with class inequality—which has proven not to be enough—but also with inequality among nations, and therefore, with the repressive machinery used to maintain both.[10] The only thing that will facilitate the operation is the fact that the power used for both purposes is one and the same—the power of the nation-state. Communism is inconceivable in a world in which discrepancies among nations in power, wealth, and development generate dominance and exploitation, rivalries and wars.

LENIN'S NEP REVISITED

Marx warned against a purely linear view of history as a cumulative chronology in which one social formation (e.g., feudalism or capitalism) supersedes another, only to produce eventually its own successor. Although in Marx's classic paradigm the conditions for revolution were created by the level of productive forces requiring a change in relations of production, there nevertheless may be historical circumstances in which the impetus of the class allows a political leap forward —a revolution, as was the case in the backward countries of Russia and China. But before long, lagging productive forces reassert their primacy, compelling the vanguard to fill the economic gap. This was precisely what Lenin had in mind when, after experimenting with various economic schemes, he inaugurated his New Economic Policy.

The question that remains relevant to this day is whether under conditions of underdevelopment the NEP is a short-term or a long-term policy. In other words, is the NEP merely a transitory phase initiated to lift Russia from the quagmire of war communism, or is it a strategy of development for the entire period of industrialization and modernization in a country that did not have the historical opportunity to go through a capitalist stage of development? I submit that the answer to this question is crucial to the current debate on the crisis besetting the USSR and Eastern Europe and that it is particularly relevant to all Third World countries choosing a noncapitalist path in their development strategy.

To find the answer, we must go back to the traumatic years of 1918-21 when, encircled by the White Armies and the troops of Japan and the Western powers, the new Soviet republic fought to survive by extending state control over all resources and economic units. Rationing, requisitioning, and primitive bartering replaced normal trade; the market ceased to exist, and money lost its value or function. The dominant feature of that period of war communism was the immobilization of economic life; the state grasped every economic lever within reach, and as a result mushroomed into a vast, cumbersome bureaucracy.

In 1921, after defeating the foreign interventionists and the White Armies, the Bolsheviks assessed the bitter fruits of victory: The country lay in ruins, national income was one-third and industrial production one-fifth of the 1913 level, the transportation system shattered, and agricultural production was so meager that the majority of the people were barely subsisting and millions of others were starving. It was against this background that Lenin announced that grain requisitioning would be replaced by a fair tax in kind, leaving all surplus produce to the individual peasant—the beginning of what would go down in history as the New Economic Policy, a radical departure from war communism.

Before going further, let me emphasize that the era of war communism—however brief and disastrous economically—has left a deep mark on the political culture of Soviet communism. War communism will stay in the minds of whole generations of Communists as the fighting period when the citadel of socialism was to be taken by storm and when almost everything —from what to eat and where to live through what to read and how to make love—was decided by the Bolsheviks. Therefore, the habits of mind and styles of action characteristic of that era—revolutionary voluntarism and elan, readiness to resort to coercion, rule by administrative fiat, and summary justice, briefly, everything that was required to get things done quickly and effectively—will linger with the generations that lived through that era and the succeeding ones that will be educated in that spirit.

As with war communism, the NEP had not been anticipated. The tax in kind was conceived as a limited step to encourage the peasant to produce and deliver a surplus on which depended the revival of industry and the cities. The original intention was to confine market relations to the "localities," which would exchange or barter goods directly with the state. But soon buying and selling swept the country and restrictions on free trade had to be removed. Gradually the tax in kind was replaced by a monetary one. In order to convince the peasant to market surplus, manufactured goods had to be offered as an incentive, and thus small enterprises were denationalized and returned to private ownership. The market evolved according to its own internal logic as nationwide free trade and market relations became the hallmark of the NEP.

By late 1923, Lenin's concept of the NEP took shape in a mixed economic system, with the state controlling the macroeconomic level and private capital predominanting in small enterprises, retail and wholesale trade, and 2 million small holdings in agriculture. In the terminology of the time, the state controlled the commanding heights—most large enterprises, particularly heavy industry, the transportation system, the banks, and the foreign trade monopoly. The predominance of the state sector in industrial production was ensured. It employed 84.1 percent of the industrial labor force, while private enterprises (though much more numerous) employed only 12.4 percent.

Lenin, emphasizing the revolutionary approach implicit in a war communism that had sought to break up the old socioeconomic system in one stroke and substitute for it a new one, pointed out that the NEP signified an abandonment of that in favor of a reformist approach, whose method was "not to break up the old socioeconomic system—trade, petty production, petty proprietorship, capitalism—but to revive trade, petty proprietorship, capitalism, while cautiously and gradually getting the upper hand over them, or making it possible to subject them to state regulation only to the extent that they revive."[11]

The central principle of the New Economic Policy was that the state, by holding a commanding position in the economy, could gradually lead the capitalist elements, particularly the peasants, toward socialism by economic means. In his famous Cooperative Plan, Lenin insisted on the need to rely on cooperatives for at least two decades, describing them as a simpler, easier, and more accessible way for the peasant to come to socialism. He emphasized that modern farming presupposes a complete cultural revolution in the village and advised that party policy must center on "peaceful, organizational cultural work" to conciliate peasant interests. Capital accumulation and industrialization, he said, must proceed on the "healthy base" of expanding market relations, with prosperous farmers joining market-oriented activities.

To impress on the party the real character of the NEP, Lenin used the concept of state capitalism present in the 1921 economy—foreign concessions, the cooperatives, private persons marketing state products, and the leasing of state property. State-owned and -operated enterprises he considered of a "consistently socialist type."[12]

In sociopolitical terms, Lenin's concept rested on the major assumption that "the social order in the Soviet republic is based on the collaboration of two classes: the workers and the peasants." Through the medium of trade, a durable economic and political *smychka* (union) between the proletariat and the peasantry, between industry and agriculture, had to be forged. Lenin was aware that such a class alignment represented a modification of classical Marxist thought; so was his emphasis on exchange and market relations. But he explained both by the fact that the first socialist revolution occurred in a backward peasant country. Where is it written, he asked rhetorically, that "such modifications of the usual historical sequence are impermissible or impossible?"[13]

The result from a theoretical viewpoint is that in a backward country that first must go through a bourgeois-democratic revolution and then must industrialize by the only method available, primitive capital accumulation, the new state power must necessarily use the economic categories that operate in such circumstances—the market, with its money-commodity relationship.

Because of the imminent pressures under which the NEP was conceived and because of the aggravation of his illness, Lenin was not specific about the duration of the NEP; in some instances he spoke of "at least two decades," in others he tried to assure his reluctant comrades it would not last too long. In fact, the NEP lasted only five years, since not until 1923 did it become a well-rounded policy.

In 1928-29, Stalin launched his "great change," which essentially signified a drastic turnabout from pragmatic policies based on a careful study of economic laws operating in the transition period to the so-called revolution from above that involved voluntary state measures to enforce rapid industrialization and forced collectivization to achieve socialism as quickly as possible.

It is characteristic of Stalin's ideological embezzlement that even after he abandoned the NEP and defeated Bukharin, its chief advocate, he continued to insist in his editorials that the "NEP is the only correct policy of socialist construction."[14] One authoritative observer writes: "Instead of transcending the NEP evolutionarily, Stalinism abolished it revolutionarily, by decree and by force. Instead of proceeding gradually and by means of persuasion, it proceeded at breakneck speed and wielded state power coercively to smash popular resistance by terrorizing the population."[15]

STALIN'S MODEL AND BUKHARIN'S ALTERNATIVE

The unbroken continuity and correct political line of the Communist party of the Soviet Union ever since it took power constitutes a leitmotiv of every party Congress, even after Stalin's death. Implicitly, the rapid industrialization, forced collectivization, and all that went with them under Stalin's rule have been integrated in the glorious history of the Communist party.

Khrushchev, after having denounced Stalin's crimes, mistakes, and abuses in a secret report to the Twentieth Congress in 1956, stated in 1961 at the Twenty-second Congress that "the Second Programme drawn up by Lenin and adopted at the Eighth Congress in 1919 for the building of a socialist society had been put into practice by the Soviet people under the leadership of the Communist party. Socialism triumphed in the Soviet Union completely and finally."[16] At the Twenty-third Congress in 1966, Leonid Brezhnev, after having in 1964 demoted Khrushchev and denounced his "adventurism and erratic behavior," stated that "all these years the CPSU (Communist Party of the Soviet Union), guided by the line laid down by the 20th, 21st and 22nd Party Congresses [all dominated by Khrushchev] has led the Soviet people unswervingly along the path of communist construction."[17]

Paradoxically, most Western experts on Soviet affairs share this view of unbroken continuity of Leninism, Bolshevism, and Stalinism and maintain that Stalinism was the inevitable outcome of the October Revolution. Philosopher Hannah Arendt, speaking at a 1967 conference devoted to that subject, summed it up: "Those who were more or less on the side of Lenin's revolution also justified Stalin, whereas those who were denouncing Stalin's rule were sure that Lenin was not only responsible for Stalin's totalitarianism but actually belongs in the same category, that Stalin was a necessary consequence of Lenin."[18]

Although it is obvious that every historical period, indeed each political phenomenon, has its seeds in the preceding one (even a revolution can be understood only in its historical context), failure to distinguish, for instance, between the French Revolution before and after Thermidor—or, for that matter, before and after Napoleon—means obscuring the very nature of the two political phenomena. In particular, I submit that the continuity thesis in the case of the Stalinist phenomenon is largely based on the underestimation of the NEP's profound and long-term significance, both economic and political, an underestimation that lumps together the two sworn enemies: official Soviet history and ideology and Western adversaries of communism. What these extreme positions have in common is the rejection of an alternative development in postrevolutionary societies—the former because its proponents thrive on perpetuation of the Stalinist power structure, the latter because they fear a more democratic and economically efficient system emerging in those societies.

In fact, there is today plenty of evidence that a completely opposite platform and program inspired by the NEP's fundamental principles, clashed in public, in the columns of *Pravda* and at party Congresses, with Stalin's strategy and model of society. Moreover, the alternative strategy elaborated by Bukharin, then editor of *Pravda*, and supported by such people as Rykov, the premier, and Tomski, the leader of the trade unions, was predominant in the party for almost five years after Lenin's death. That out of the long list of Stalin's victims the name of the spokesman of that alternative strategy, N. I. Bukharin, has never been rehabilitated, his works and ideas never mentioned in official documents or in the literature and mass media—all of this should give a clue to the present status of Stalinism in the USSR and in Eastern Europe. Therefore, I propose to refresh memories by showing that in the formative stages of the Soviet model there was a clash between competing forces and viewpoints on various issues of development, some of which retain their relevance today.

The crux of the matter in industrialization is what Marx used to call capital accumulation, the transformation of part of the economic surplus into additional capital indispensable to enlarging production by building industry. How and where to get it when there was very little surplus? That was the first question that sharply divided the Bolshevik party.

The Sources of Accumulation

E. Preobrazhenskii, the leading Soviet economist in the 1920s, was the first to attack this sensitive issue head-on.[19] Arguing that in a socialist country neither colonialist loot, big loans, nor returns from foreign credits were available, he formulated the law of "primitive socialist accumulation," suggesting rather bluntly the need to expand the industrial capital rapidly, at the expense of the peasant sector. Eventually, Stalin decided to base his policy on that law without acknowledging it. Since Marx had described primitive accumulation as "systematic plundering" of noncapitalist economic forms, acquiring surplus capital by "compulsion and robbery," Stalin dropped the first part of capital accumulation (speaking only of "accumulation") and coined a more convenient ideological formula, "the socialist method of industrialization," claiming it was different from the capitalist method. We are reminded of a similar ideological embezzlement: Stalin's theory that the world market had split into a capitalist world market and a socialist one. Actually, these formulas were designed to conceal the fact that the Soviet state was compelled to use capitalist methods in both cases.

Bukharin, who had vacillated earlier on the issues of the New Economic Policy, rejected Preobrazhenskii's theory not only on economic grounds but also, on political and moral grounds. He argued that such a policy would alienate the peasantry and undermine the *smychka*, thus endangering the regime. Because he considered the issue to be relevant to all backward peasant countries, he added that industrialization based on the exploitation of peasantry was also wrong from the perspective of world revolution. Although Bukharin agreed that Soviet industrialization would have to rely mainly on a transfer from the agrarian sector (a limited and carefully conducted transfer, he insisted), his emphasis was on making industrial growth dependent on an expanding consumer market. In short, he said the situation in industry cannot be viewed independently of the growth of productive forces in agriculture and that accumulation in socialist industry cannot occur for long without accumulation in the peasant sector. In other words, Bukharin tied the issue of accumulation primarily to the growth of agricultural production.[20]

The issue of accumulation has vast sociopolitical implications regarding class policy. It involves both the distribution of investments in heavy industry versus agriculture and consumer goods and the method of that distribution. Whereas Stalin accompanied his program of heavy industrialization—funded by tribute-like extraction from the peasantry—with an intensified class war, recurrent "extraordinary measures," and increased repression, Bukharin revealed the potential tyranny in such an economic option. Bukharin advocated economic means to stimulate the workers and to attract the cooperation of peasants, revolutionary legality rather than arbitrariness and coercion. Under his plan the party was to abandon force as its modus operandi and was to use persuasion in dealing with the working masses. Hence, this fundamental division on economic policy involved class interests and certainly political differences.

Collective Farms or Cooperatives

Already in the second half of the 1920s a striking imbalance appeared in the development of industry and agriculture—an imbalance that to this day has remained the weakest point of Soviet economic policy. I submit that although the ruthless and coercive methods used in grain procurement and collectivization left deep scars among the peasantry, they cannot alone explain a failure of such magnitude and duration. After all, over the years dozens of plenary meetings of the Central Committee and many government decisions have dealt with such abuses and mistakes in agriculture, each time prescribing measures to eliminate the abuses and remedy the mistakes. There must be something much deeper, something at the very roots of farm production, to explain why a country with such a vast area of arable land (230 million hectares compared to 185 million hectares in the United States) should be compelled to spend billions of dollars annually to import grains, butter, and meat at a time when quite a few industrial nations have succeeded in becoming self-sufficient in such vital products.

It has been proven in the United States and other leading grain-producing nations that a significant increase in grain output depends on modern farming techniques, most of which are best used in large-scale farming. This is a lesson for any developing country. The subsistence peasant in backward areas does not have the means to acquire modern techniques, nor would the peasant be able to employ them on dwarf plots. Therefore, large-scale farming is a prerequisite of highly efficient grain production. How to arrive at it?

This was a much-disputed issue in the Bolshevik party. Although the discussion was marred by peasant resistance, threat of famile, kulak uprisings, and the overall class warfare climate fomented by Stalin and his "forced marches," the initial choice was between cooperative functioning on the basis of economic incentives and market relations and kolkhoz (collective farms) in which the emphasis was on organized production by quasi-military mobilization and socialist emulation directed from above—all subordinated to the central plan. In fact, the kolkhoz works like a state enterprise: It must produce what the plan orders it to produce and then sell to the state most of its output at prices set by the state.

Stalin, although often quoting Lenin, initiated an agriculture policy that was dominated by his impatient drive for quick collectivization, his belief in administrative fiat, and the mobilization of the party on the agricultural front to eliminate the kulaks and destroy them as a class. He presented this scheme as a military offensive in the revolutionary heroic tradition of the October takeover and the valiant battles of the civil war.

Bukharin opposed such a policy, recalling Lenin's plan to bring the peasant to socialism through cooperatives based on marketing, buying, and credit. Circulation, he argued, is the high road of agriculture to socialism. Through the struggle on the market, through competition, state and cooperative enterprises would oust their private competitors; and, in the end, would eliminate the market itself. Such was the dialectical strategy advocated by Bukharin.[21]

Economic versus Administrative Means

If I had to use one key word to describe Bukharin's approach to agriculture, I would settle for "economic" means as opposed to Stalin's fanatical belief in "administrative" methods accompanied by party mobilization and socialist emulation. (Every season the party must organize campaigns for the peasants on how to sow, weed, and harvest—a method that has been going on to this day.) In fact, this fundamental difference extended throughout the range of options in economic policy with their social and political implications. Thus, Bukharin's concept of the NEP should be viewed as a distinct alternative to Stalinism. It is pertinent here to quote the authoritative characterization of his biographer:

Developing the themes of Lenin's last writings, which constituted both a defense and further elaboration of NEP as a road to socialism and adding some of his own, Bukharin became the party's main theorist of NEP. Though his policies evolved between 1924 and 1928 toward great emphasis on planning, heavy industrial investment, and efforts to promote a partial and voluntary farm sector, he remained committed to the NEP economic framework of a state, or "socialist" sector (mainly large-scale industry, transportation and banking) and a private sector (peasant farm and small manufacturing, trade and service enterprises) interacting through market relations. Even during the crisis of 1928-29, NEP was for Bukharinists a viable development (not static) model, predicated on civil peace, that could reconcile Bolshevik aspirations and Russian reality.[22]

Stalin's plan for industry was a command-type system with highly centralized decision-making power at the top and administrative allocation of resources. True, in the early industrialization phases when the objective was rather limited–to build a technical-industrial foundation–this plan proved effective in promoting economic growth. These phases involved a simple set of priorities: an energy base, machine tools, metallurgical and armament industries, and a physical infrastructure, particularly transportation. Within such a narrow area the process was self-feeding: more mining to extract mineral ores, more iron ore to produce steel, to produce more machines, to build more blast furnaces, and so on. It was then possible to make decisions at the top and to direct resources in a few selected areas.

Moreover, the revolutionary spirit was still high among the working class; party mobilization and socialist emulation could be used as substitutes for material incentives as long as the tens of millions of workers coming from the rural areas felt that improvement in their living conditions was under way. Besides, wherever mobilization and emulation failed, stern penalties and repressive measures helped to discipline the workers.

Those were the five-year plans of spectacular achievements. The rates of Soviet industrial growth from the thirties to World War II increased more than 18 percent annually, nearly twice the rates during boom periods in capitalist countries at the time of their industrialization. The growth was particularly impressive in global quantitative terms, with the Soviet Union becoming the greatest world producer in oil, pig iron and steel, iron and manganese ore, cement, timber, cotton, wool, and so on. However, given the advanced state of scientific knowledge in the world and the high investment rates, actual productivity remained considerably low in most industrial sectors, and low also was the quality of industrial products.

Now, keeping in mind the discussion and division in the party in the twenties and thirties, a legitimate question arises: Why did Stalin's strategy prevail? I submit that the socioeconomic conditions of backwardness constitute only the background against which a satisfactory answer can be found, because those same conditions did not and could not prevent the alternative strategy from taking shape in the highest echelons of the Bolshevik party and to dominate for almost a decade the official ideology and propaganda of the regime. Recall that during that period Bukharin was a Politburo member, editor of *Pravda*, head of the Comintern, and chief theoretician and for three years co-leader with Stalin of the Communist party, while his closest associates, Rykov and Tomski, held the powerful positions of premier and union leader, respectively.

Therefore, one must also consider the political tradition and culture—the harsh political climate of the civil war and foreign intervention, the traumatic years of war communism and capitalist encirclement that established in the party a tradition of martial defiance and heroism in the face of formidable odds. Under such conditions, the party's democratic norms and practice of clashing views (Lenin was twice in a minority position in the Central Committee) gave way to a rigid authoritarianism and pervasive militarization of life on every level.

What used to be public debate with conflicting views aired in *Pravda* and other party publications was confined to the party hierarchy and acquired a covert nature, keeping the entire exchange of ideas about the best way to build socialism far from the working class and the nation at large. In the process, all the forms of popular power, from the local soviets to factory committees, were transformed into appendages of the central power. The ever-present threat of imperialist aggression that became increasingly perceptible with Hitler's advent to power in Germany generated in the party a propensity for willful and energetic courses of action rather than for the kind of rational, prudent, and painstaking approach advocated by Bukharin. Political will rather than due consideration to economic categories and laws became the criterion of economic policy.

It was this heroic tradition and harsh political climate that Stalin, in control of the party Secretariat, skillfully manipulated, gradually building his tremendous power base in the party machinery and eliminating every challenge to his authority, ultimately leaving his mark on the entire system. Stalin's became the party line, the strategy of industrialization and collectivization, the organization of a power structure with all decision-making power and political initiative concentrated at the top. This model subsequently expanded throughout Eastern Europe.

Obviously, Stalinism responds to the specific aims of the party apparat, which sees in planning and in administrative methods the safest way to acquire and consolidate power. We are thus dealing with a self-fulfilling and reinforcing esprit de corps that explains both the strength and resilience of Stalinism long after the death of its maker. However, fundamental in the definition of Stalinism are the production relations upon which it was built—that is, the essential social relations peculiar to its formation. It is the system of these relations that influences, in the last analysis, the economic, political, and ideological features of the society. What are they?

I submit that these production relations cannot be described either as capitalist (state capitalism, as some authors view them) or socialist (the official claim); nor are we dealing here with a new mode of production, which some authors label collectivist. Rather it is a combination of elements typical of a transition period in which the old relations have not been totally eliminated while the new ones are still struggling to assert themselves—elements proper to socialism, to capitalism, and, perhaps the most characteristic, to precapitalism. Indeed, the 1917 Revolution implanted in Russia a postcapitalist class structure in an economy that was precapitalist with respect to its productive forces in general and to agriculture in particular, with the latter being predominant both economically and socially.

To start with, production relations were socialist in that private ownership of the means of production was abolished; and so was private buying of labor power, implicitly private accumulation of the surplus product, empowering the state to act as the owner and manager of the means of production. Production relations are capitalist in that the regime had to maintain the economic incentive of the sale of labor power—the producer of the surplus for capital accumulation so indispensable to industrialization; moreover, both the norms of retribution and the distribution system remained bourgeois, as Marx had so clearly anticipated. As for the precapitalist production relations, those are still in place in the fact that production, consumption, and wages are all regulated by extra-economic coercion.

Thus, if the social background of Stalinism is to be identified, it is the precapitalist social relations that we must examine. As one author put it: "Stalinism is the elimination of precapitalism as regards production technology founded on an anticapitalist form of ownership and precapitalist pattern for organizing production relations and political power. The roots of this precapitalism are, for the most part, to be found in the regime's economic functions: the direct use of extra-economic coercion in regulating production relations."[23] This is certainly a feature inherited from feudal Russia, and it is this feature that became decisive in the way Stalin would organize political power and mold ideology. Here are the roots of Stalin's command-type planning system and of the administrative method of enforcing it.

It is in this context that scholarly endeavors to find patterns in the political culture of Russian prerevolutionary history to explain Stalin's inclination for etatism, administrative methods, and Great Russian nationalism become significant. As one writer put it: "Stalinist revolutionism from above had a prehistory in the political culture of Russian tsarism, it existed as a pattern in the Russian past and hence could be seen by a twentieth-century statesman as both a precedent and legitimation of a political course that would, in essentials, recapitulate the historical pattern."[24] This has been well documented by the legalized imposition of serfdom on the Russian peasantry in the sixteenth and seventeenth centuries: the peasant's attachment by law to the soil, together with the system of *barshchina*, under which the peasant was bound to contribute a certain number of days of work on the landowner's (or state's) land during the agricultural year. The Russian village commune was transformed by the government into a coercive organization for ensuring each member's fulfillment of state-imposed obligations under the principle of mutual responsibility (*krugovaia poruka*).

All these facts caused the Russian historian Pavel Miliukov to note as early as 1904 that "in Russia the state exerted enormous influence upon the social organization whereas in the West the social organization conditioned the state system."[25] The coercive organization and the state-imposed obligations bear a striking resemblance to Stalin's concept of the kolkhoz —his harsh law compelling the kolkhoz to surrender annually a major part of the produce to the state at very low prices— and the "mutual responsibility" so often invoked by Stalin in justifying his agricultural policies.

Other historians draw an interesting parallel between Stalin's industrialization drive and the transformation of Russian society and development of its economic base for state-ordained purposes that was initiated by Peter I—that "crowned revolutionary," as Herzen called him. Of course, the ever-swelling bureaucracy that became so powerful and indispensable under Stalin was bearing marks whose historical roots could be traced back to the czarist *chinovnik* and its ubiquitous presence in Russian nineteenth-century society.[26]

In summary, the coexistence within the economy of elements, not only contradictory but at times incompatible, created conditions for political power to play a direct role in the management of the economy. Political power was given the task of managing conflicting economic laws and tendencies and of compelling them to adjust their workings within the national economy. Hence, politics became an integral part of the economic process; without it, the economic system could not function. Clearly such a system gets weary and, as we will see, has no longevity.

REFORM THE ECONOMY WITHOUT REALLY TRYING

Stalin died at a time when the Soviet economy was beginning to falter. Because Stalin's death produced a dislocation in the power structure, the logic of politics required his ambitious successors to provide a more or less articulated alternative to his harsh and ruthless reign. Malenkov and, later, Khrushchev were clearly driven by this logic.

The last five-year plan with a high rate of growth (13.2 percent) was that of 1950-54. The decline started slowly, but in 1961 the Soviet economy suffered its first major setback, with industrial growth dropping by 4 percent. At the same time, Soviet agriculture was at an impasse. Grain output and cattle production remained stagnant. For the first time true statistics were made public, revealing the appalling performance of what Stalin used to call "the most advanced agriculture in the world." Forty years after the Revolution, the second world power could not feed its people.

Khrushchev viewed the situation as the result of the repressive administrative policies of Stalin, and he took swift measures to eliminate some of their effects. The forced labor camps were dismantled, the severe penalties in factories were abolished, and unions were given the right to control dismissals, norms, wage tariffs, and so on. In 1957, he created *sovnarkhozy*, administrative units on a territorial basis—a departure from the specialized management of branches directed by ministries. However, the new management system did not amount to real decentralization; central planning remained strong, specifying thirty to forty binding rules for enterprises. Moreover, the compromise caused such irregularities in the functioning of the economy that in 1966 the previous specialized management system had to be restored.

In agricultural policy, Khrushchev seemed to act with greater determination. He formally abolished the law compelling the kolkhoz to surrender annually a major part of their produce to the state at very low prices; instead, higher prices were offered to stimulate production, tractors and machinery were sold to the kolkhoz, and the kolkhoz were encouraged to organize workshops and produce construction materials, tools, food products, and so on. As a result, the output of meat, milk, and butter increased rapidly (meat from 5.4 million tons in 1953 to 5.9 million tons in 1957 and milk from 13.7 million tons in 1953 to 23.5 million tons in 1957). However, grain production fell short of the 1960 target to only 180 million tons.

The condition that prevented Khrushchev from making public the Twentieth Congress speech denouncing Stalin's appalling abuses and crimes forced him to stop short of initiating the kind of structural changes in the planning and management system that were required to make the economy function under the new conditions. The condition was the resistance of the party apparat. In fact, it is difficult to credit Khrushchev with developing a coherent and all-encompassing scheme for economic reform for the simple reason that such a radical measure necessarily required drastic changes in the political system. And here was his Achilles' heel: Khrushchev was not prepared to go the whole hog because he remained a staunch advocate of highly centralized power, and he certainly exercised and enjoyed it every minute.

Nevertheless, he emphasized two principles implicit in such economic reform: the need to use material incentives to stimulate production and the idea of partial economic decentralization. There is plenty of evidence that the other members of the Politburo were reluctant to adopt even these two principles, as shown by the cautious way in which they mentioned them in their public pronouncements. Even after the June 1957 crisis, which ended with the elimination of the "anti-party group" (Malenkov, Kaganovitch, and Molotov; Shepilov, having been charged with joining the group; and Saburov and Pervukhin, with no explanation), the majority of the Politburo opposed reform.

Perhaps even more convincing in this respect is the fact that after Khrushchev's downfall, the leadership derided his emphasis on material incentives and well-being as "goulash communism," and most of the decentralization measures, however timid and inconsistent, were rescinded.

Stepanov, the editor in chief of *Communist*, made this typical comment: "To equate communism with the mere fulfillment of the 'stomach's needs,' with a narrow, blind practical approach when we are facing the wide horizons of the future and higher ideals would be profoundly wrong" (Pravda, 17 May 1965).

Therefore, I submit that despite the official reason given for Khrushchev's demotion (his "erratic and adventurist behavior," which can be fully documented), the underlying factor that lent political clout to the coup was the stubborn resistance of the party apparat to all his attempts to curtail its privileged position of power and control over the economy as sanctified in the Stalinist model. Only on such a solid political base could the members of the Politburo stage the coup successfully.

It is useful to pursue this point more deeply because it reveals the political articulations of the economic reform and the way the Soviet power mechanism has been reacting to change to this day. In 1957, three years after he was appointed first secretary, Khrushchev was confronted with the first challenge to his leadership. Additional facts divulged later show that the challenge came not only from the antiparty group of Malenkov, Kaganovitch, and Molotov—accused in the Central Committee resolution of June 22-29, 1957 of having opposed a series of decisions during the previous three or four years[27] —but also by Shepilov, charged with having joined the group; Saburov and Pervukhin; the head of the government, Bulganin; and the chief of state, Voroshilov. That is, no fewer than seven out of eleven Presidium members tried to expel Khrushchev from his post as party leader. He managed to save his position only by convening in great haste a plenary session of the Central Committee that reversed the Presidium's decision and reinstated him as leader of the party.

Recall that the political crisis had been preceded by Khrushchev's swift measures to eliminate Stalinist repressive policies, and by such initiatives as the campaign for the cultivation of virgin lands, abolition of a number of industrial ministries, and creation of regional economic councils (*sovnarkhozy*), not to mention the 1956 secret report at the Twentieth Congress on "the cult of personality and its consequences."

Although his June victory over his adversaries had been complete, Khrushchev dealt gradually and prudently with them, one at a time, which shows that the opposition group had a political base in the party that he did not want to antagonize. It took more than a year to demote Bulganin as head of government, Pervukhin and Saburov were implicated in the antiparty group only in 1959, and Voroshilov, still chief of state, was accused much later at the Twenty-second Congress, in October 1961. Another indication of the strength of the opposition's political base was the abnormal circumstance in Soviet political life that the membership of the Central Committee had not changed in the four years that had elapsed since the Twentieth Congress in 1956, although in the meantime the balance of power at the top looked different. Studies reveal that of the 309 participants in the June plenary session of 1957, nearly 100 found it imprudent to take a stand on the leadership issue.

After Khrushchev's downfall, the party apparat—shaken, humiliated, and confined to administrative tasks—began a fierce struggle to regain its traditional politico-ideological prerogatives. The first major decision of the new collective leadership was to rescind the 1962 reform by reuniting the agricultural and industrial branches of the apparat. The *oblast, raykom,* and *gorkom* (Russian administrative units) committees were reinstated so that the apparat regained the form it had enjoyed for more than forty years; the first secretary of these committees recovered his status as a local leader and also saw the familiar chain of command restored.

Then another demand of the *apparatchiki,* job security, was met. Although the party statute of 1961 providing for the "systematic renewal of cadres" could not be amended immediately, new instructions were sent in September 1965, on the occasion of elections held for the lower echelon committees in preparation for the party Congress, emphasizing the "need to maintain experienced cadres in Party work and to respect the principles of continuity in leadership."[28] Small wonder that the Congress flattered the "experienced cadres" of the Stalinist era and canceled the rule of "systematic renewal of cadres" in the party statute, thus satisfying the yearning for tenure and stability so characteristic of the party cadres.

However, the party apparat (like the top leadership) should not be regarded as a bloc or a homogeneous entity. There are tensions between various levels of the party bureaucracy, particularly between the central apparat and the rest, some of which had clearly surfaced after Stalin's death. The large group of party activists headed by Khrushchev and made up of representatives of a new generation that grew up under historical conditions quite different from the years of civil war and capitalist encirclement was leaning toward new economic policies. The emerging political force within the party that favored change and also struggled for power began by denouncing Stalin's crimes publicly, allowing accounts of the concentration camps to be published, encouraging historical analyses of Stalin's strategic mistakes at the beginning of the war, and even permitting criticism of the rigid command-type planning system. But they stopped short of a critical analysis of the Stalinist class base and power structure. The fundamental causes that permitted, indeed favored, such a monstrous regime to emerge and govern the country for so long were sidestepped; and so was the deformation of socialist ideology to fit that regime. Neither Khrushchev nor his followers were prepared to accept the radical conclusion of such in-depth analysis of the political system.

The forces for change in the party, particularly the intelligentsia and the managers of economic enterprises, continued to seek political representation even after Khrushchev's downfall. This time the leading reformer was Kosygin. In his first speech as prime minister, he said rather emphatically, "We cannot hope to exceed the high productivity reached by most developed capitalist countries unless we increase the worker's initiative and freedom of action."[29] With his blessing, articles by advocates of "Libermanism" multiplied in the press along with countless critiques of managers shackled by rigid controls.

It is necessary to recall at this point the vivid discussion among Soviet economists that took place in 1962 in the propitious climate of the thaw created by Khrushchev's initiatives. The economist Y. G. Liberman was the first to pinpoint the contradiction between measures designed to stimulate industrial production and the numerous binding rules imposed on enterprises by Gosplan, the state planning commission. In his famous 1955 article, he advocated a larger autonomy for enterprises and a flexible system of management.[30] In practice, he suggested the introduction of profit incentives to encourage managers to set and attain higher output targets, to introduce technological innovations and new products, and to improve the overall quality of products. Through such a program workers were supposed to become interested in the affairs and success of the factory.

During the summer of 1964 an experimental program was begun in a clothing factory and a shoemaking factory: Bolshevichka in Moscow and Mayak in Gorki. On 12 October 1964, two days before Khrushchev's downfall, a *Pravda* editorial stated: "This experiment deserves wider application, not only within the ready-make clothing industry, but also in other branches of light industry." Indeed, the experiment resulted in startling results, surpassing the most optimistic expectations. Kosygin himself deplored the fact that the few rights granted earlier to the enterprises were "still far from being fully exercised."[31] However, the Liberman experiment was silently killed by the powerful forces in the party that resisted change.

As the Soviet economy continued its decline, Prime Minister Kosygin initiated in 1965-66 a series of measures designed to release enterprises from some of the heaviest administrative burdens. The plan reduced thirty to forty of the rules imposed on enterprises to eight (basic goods to be produced, capital investment, production to be sold, tasks regarding new equipment, technical-material supply, level of profits and income, total wage fund, and payments to be made to the budget. Enterprises were given the right to refuse useless and excessive supplies by warning the supplier with a ten-day notice. Firms could modify the conditions of the contracts when this did not interfere with the realization of the plan. Although these measures never challenged the dominant position of Gosplan, they nevertheless were perceived as opening the door for a decentralization process.

A fierce but muted struggle took place around them. Kosygin made a speech in which he recalled Lenin's indication that Gosplan should enjoy a certain independence, a certain autonomy, and he did not mention the usual sacred reference points: ideology, communism, or even the party. The text was ignored by the major papers, and it was published after a month's delay in Gosplan's monthly journal. Various articles in *Pravda* and *Kommunist*, however, indirectly rejected the idea of Gosplan autonomy, reiterating the leading role of the party in both the planning and management system.

Kosygin fought back as the Presidium met in Moscow in mid-May 1965, and as a result a strong editorial appeared in *Izvestia* (May 21) ostensibly aimed at the antireform movement. It sharply condemned "subjectivism, willful decisions and ignorance of economic laws in the management of the economy...the Party confirmed once again that it is the economic methods of management of socialist production that preserve the basic meaning and best ensure the development of the worker's initiative." It went further: "The March (1965) plenary session of the Central Committee devoted its chief attention to the reinforcement of profit incentives in the development of production and the consolidation of the financial basis of agriculture."

Michel Tatu, who was then in Moscow as correspondent of *Le Monde*, noted that it was then up to *Pravda* to reply.[32] An article by Laszlo Osrban written in just the right vein warned: "Further progress depends not only on solving economic problems but also on the results of ideological and educational work. If the principle of profit incentives is envisaged unilaterally...this will give rise to a selfishness that is alien to socialism" (*Pravda*, 21 May 1965), as though the emphasis on ideologico-educational work in the Stalinist era had abolished selfishness!

An indication as to who was behind these antireform attacks came with the victory celebration in May 1965. In his main report, Brezhnev came out publicly for acclaim of Stalin, "the Secretary General of the Party who was at the head of the State Committee for Defense," making an apparent effort to depict Stalin's entire policy as beyond reproach from beginning to end. An article in *Pravda* by S. P. Trapeznikov, appointed by Brezhnev as the new head of the Central Committee Department of Science and Education, took another step in that direction: "The period of the struggle for the industrialization of the country, for the socialist transformation of the village, and for the cultural revolution was one of the most brilliant in the history of the Party and the Soviet State. It was a period of rich experience in theoretical and practical Party activities, a hard fought struggle for ideological purity within its ranks, and the education of communists in the spirit of unconditional faithfulness to Marxism-Leninism" (8 October 1965). This time not only were Stalin's achievements clearly acclaimed, but also his ideological purges, the killing of so many poets, writers, artists, and the like.

Such speeches and articles alarmed the forces resisting a return to Stalinism. Letters, petitions, and memoranda signed by personalities, academics, writers, and artists were addressed to the leadership protesting the maneuvers trying to rehabilitate Stalin.[33]

At the Twenty-third Congress in 1966, Brezhnev, while assuming the title of secretary-general, glossed over the whole issue. Stalin and the "cult" were not mentioned at all; Khrushchev was not mentioned either, and the language used when dealing with his "mistakes" was restrained. There was only one speech by Yegorychev, the Moscow secretary, that censured the "cult of personality, the violation of Leninist standards and principles in the life of the Party" on the one hand and rejected "all attempts to suppress the heroic history of our people" during those years on the other hand—a sort of neither-nor approach to the whole problem, with which the collective leadership was closing the matter.[34]

In cultural affairs, the Twenty-third Congress constituted a triumph for the conservatives. All institutions of an ideological character (radio, television, cinema, publishing, and cultural relations with foreign countries) were withdrawn from government jurisdiction and placed under direct party authority. Some old-time Stalinist planners (e.g., Baybakov, Antonov, and Matskevich) were given back their jobs in the government, and a number of high-ranking cadres were transferred from party to government jobs. These measures were meant to strengthen the party's grip on the state.

Thus, the 1970s were the golden era for the apparat, years of consolidation and stability for the whole political system. An absolute consensus prevailed over the relations between the leadership and the apparat of the party, whose domination and control over the economy were undisputed.[35]

NOTES

1. I. V. Stalin, *Pravda*, 30 April 1924; and *Ob Osnovakh Leninizma* (Moscow, 1924), 60.

2. Predominant in Stalin's definition of the socialist state was the class-theoretical determination of the state. This neglected its economic underpinning—that is, the effect upon the form of the state of the process of capital accumulation. Lenin warned that during the first phase

one would have to preserve "not only the bourgeois right but even the bourgeois state—without the bourgeoisie" (*Statul si Revolutia Editura P.C.R.*, 1946, 107). Only this form of state could handle capital accumulation, extract it from the peasantry and working class, and use the economic surplus to enlarge production while keeping consumption low. This is essentially a bourgeois function, and one should view it in the context of industrialization, which historically belongs to the capitalist stage; it is the bourgeoisie that has developed the theory of industrialization and the ways and means to implement it. Therefore, as we will see later, to carry out industrialization successfully the state must skillfully use the economic categories that operate during that stage, as Lenin began doing in 1921 with the NEP.

3. K. Marx, *Critique of the Gotha Program* (Bucharest: Editura Politica, 1956).

4. Ibid.

5. I. V. Stalin, "The International Character of the October Revolution" *Pravda*, 6-7 November 1927.

6. V. I. Lenin, *Collected Works*, vol. 31 (Moscow 1966), 148.

7. I. V. Stalin, *Probleme Economice ale Socialismului*, (Bucharest: Editura pentru Literatura Politica, 1952), 70-71.

8. During the 1969 Moscow Symposium on the theory of international relations, the Soviet historian V. Gantman had this to say: "In my opinion, the relations between the two socio-economic systems in the world arena, if we may put it that way, run deeper than the system of international relations, inasmuch as the struggle between these two systems is not waged only in the sphere of international relations" ("The Class-Nature of Present Day International Relations," *Mejhdunarodnyi Jhizn*, September 1969). His assumption is that the class-ideological conflict is stronger than the conflicts characteristic of the interstate system. However, how can we then explain that in all the instances mentioned at the beginning of this chapter—particularly in the relations among the United States, the USSR, and China—strategic considerations clearly override ideological ones? I submit that Gantman's thesis is valid only at the national level, where the class struggle is the decisive motive force, whereas at the international level, motive forces generated by the interstate system prevail.

9. See Immanuel Wallerstin, "Crisis in Transition," in *Dynamics of Global Crisis* (New York: Monthly Review, 1982).

10. See S. Brucan, *The Dissolution of Power* (New York: Knopf, 1971).

11. V. I. Lenin, "Our Revolution" in *The Lenin Anthology*, Robert Tucker, ed. (New York: Norton 1971).

12. V. I. Lenin, *On Cooperatives* (Bucharest: Editura de Stat pentru Literatura Politica, 1955).

13. V. I. Lenin, *Opere*, vol. 32 (Bucharest: Editura Politica, 1965), 215.

14. See *Pravda* 28 April 1919 and 21 March 1931.

15. See "Stalinism as Revolution from Above" in *Stalinism*, Robert Tucker, ed. (New York: Norton, 1977); and E. J. Carr, *The Interregnum 1923-1924* (New York: Penguin, 1954).

16. Program of the CPSU (Moscow, 1961).

17. The Twenty-third Congress of the CPSU (Moscow, 1966).

18. See Richard Pipes, ed., *Revolutionary Russia* (Cambridge Mass.: Cambridge University Press, 1968), 345; see also Isaac Deutscher, *Stalin* (New York: Vintage Press, 1960).

19. E. Preobrazhenskii, *Osnovoi zakon sotsialisticheskogo nakoplenia* (The Fundamental Law of Socialist Accumulation) Kn. 8 (Moscow: Kommunisticheskaia Akademiia, Vestnik, 1924), 47-116.

20. Nikolai Bukharin, *Put'k sotsializmu i raboche-krestianskii soiuz* (The Path to Socialism and the Worker-Peasant Union) (Moscow: 1925).

21. Stephen F. Cohen, *Bukharin and the Bolshevik Revolution* (New York: Knopf, 1973).

22. Stephen F. Cohen, "Bolshevism and Stalinism," in *Stalinism*, Robert Tucker, ed. (New York: Norton, 1977), 22.

23. Felice Garcia Casals, *The Syncretic Society* (Armonk, N.Y.: Sharpe, 1981).

24. Robert Tucker, ed., *Stalinism* (New York: Norton, 1973), 95.

25. P. Miliukov, *Ocherkipo istorii russkoi kul'tury*, 5th ed. (St. Petersburg: 1904).

26. See also Moshe Lewin, *Political Undercurrents in Soviet Economic Debate: From Bukharin to Modern Reformers* (Princeton, N.J., 1974); Robert Tucker, ed., *Stalin as Revolutionary 1879-1929* (New York, 1973); Roy Medvedev, *Let History Judge: The Origin and Consequences of Stalinism* (New York: Knopf, 1971); Roy Medvedev, *On Socialist Democracy* (New York, 1975); Tony Cliff, *State Capitalism in*

Russia (London, 1974); Joseph Berliner, *Factory and Manager in the USSR* (Cambridge, Mass.: Cambridge University Press), Robert V. Daniels, *The Conscience of the Revolution* (Cambridge, Mass., 1965); Hannah Arendt, *The Origins of Totalitarianism* (New York: Harcourt Brace, 1951); Alec Nove, *Was Stalin Really Necessary?* (London, 1964); James Kuhlman, *The Foreign Policies of Eastern Europe* (Leyden, Netherlands, 1978); and, in particular, James Kuhlman, "Eastern Europe," in *World Politics*, James Rosenau, ed. (New York: Free Press, 1976), Moshe Lewin, *The Making of the Soviet System* (New York: Pantheon Books, 1985); and Stephen F. Cohen, *Rethinking the Soviet Experience* (Oxford University Press, 1985).

27. *Pravda*, 4 July 1957.

28. *Partyinaya Zhizn*, no. 17 (1965): 7.

29. *Pravda*, 20 October 1964.

30. Y. G. Liberman, "Khozyaistvennye raschot i materialnoya zainteresovannost rabotnikov promyshlennosti," *Voprosy Ekonomiki*, no. 6 (1955).

31. *Izvestia*, 21 May 1965.

32. Michel Tatu, *Power in the Kremlin from Khrushchev to Kosygin* (New York: Viking Press, 1970); see also Edward Crankshaw, *Khrushchev's Russia* (London: Penguin, 1959).

33. *Pravda* 8 October 1965.

34. Quoted in Tatu, *Power in the Kremlin*, 489.

35. The conservatism and petrification of the political structure of the Brezhnev era were reflected in the recurrent message that not only would there be no change in policies but there would also be no change in personnel, except those dictated by natural biological limits.

Interestingly, and quite understandably, the rate of personnel change in the apparat has been diminishing in inverse proportion to the advancing age of the top leadership. In 1964, when Khrushchev was demoted, the average age of the Politburo member was 54; in 1981, at the Twenty-sixth Party Congress, the average age was 71. Thus leadership reelection steadily increased throughout the Brezhnev era, advancing from a reelection rate of 73 percent in 1966 (Twenty-fourth Congress) to 83 percent in 1976 (Twenty-fifth Congress) and 100 percent in 1981 (Twenty-sixth Congress). Typical of that system of virtual life peerage is the following case: As Kosygin presented his resignation after two heart attacks that kept him out of office as prime minister for three and six months, respectively, the Politburo rejected his offer to resign. Apparently, his old comrades were afraid to set such a precedent: resignation on the ground of illness. In fact, most of them were sick, and some had also had strokes.

Within the same period (1965-81) only twelve of the fifty-eight ministers and deputy chairmen of the Council of Ministers had retired or been removed, despite the fact that the survivors averaged 70 years of age; a similar low rate of personnel turnover prevailed after the Twenty-third Party Congress in 1966 in the central apparat of the party. Eighty-nine percent of those elected to the Central Committee at the Twenty-fourth Congress were reelected five years later at the Twenty-fifth Congress, although the average age of the Central Committee's membership in 1977 was 66.

Actually, if there was some personnel change in that seventeen-year period of stability, it resulted chiefly from death or retirement. Twenty-six of the government officials and central party apparat officers had died in office, and an additional ten retired on pension.

The picture changes quite drastically for key posts at the local level. The main explanation is that the old guard had moved to the center of power and therefore a strong rejuvenation of cadres became a must; as a result, the postwar generation controls most of the local key positions at the regional and county levels of the party. This tells something about the future, since the local first secretaries traditionally constitute the pool out of which the men for the higher positions in the party are recruited. It is worth mentioning that approximately 70 percent of all current party members joined the party after 1952, yet only 15 percent of the Central Committee in 1982 came from this generation.

2

THE PRESENT

THE TURNING POINT: THE SCIENTIFIC-TECHNOLOGICAL REVOLUTION

As long as the main task was to overcome underdevelopment and as long as the sources of quantitative growth—labor, capital, land, and natural resources—were abundant, the Stalinist economic system based on command-type planning, decision-making concentrated at the top, and administrative means to enforce decisions assured high rates of economic growth and spectacular performances in industrial, quantitative terms. The Soviet Union became the world's second largest economy after the United States and the largest producer of steel, oil, iron ore, cement, coal, and cotton. The other East European countries also achieved tremendous progress toward industrialization, reaching growth rates almost twice as high as those in Western Europe for more than two decades. As a result, the economic gap with the West was narrowing, the socialist countries were successfully catching up with capitalism.

However, as early as the sixties the lower performance of the Soviet economy was signaling that the ability to increase quantity was no longer possible (as in the case of labor) and no longer effective (as in the case of capital). What was now required to spur growth was an increase in the quality of the product, a type of growth that can be achieved by improving production efficiency through modern organization and management techniques. The essential element in this type of growth is the continual introduction of modern technology. Thus, the economy had to pass from extensive growth to intensive growth.

This coincided with the major postwar economic boom in the West, when a series of scientific breakthroughs began to be incorporated on a large scale into industrial technology. The available data show that in all Western countries the technological revolution resulted in considerable expansion of productive forces, beginning with the United States and followed by the West German and Italian "miracles" in the sixties and the record-breaking achievements of Japan in the seventies and early eighties. Even moderately industrialized countries like Spain and Greece jumped 8 to 10 percent in economic growth once they introduced the new technologies in their industrial processes.

It was precisely at this point that the USSR and, subsequently, all East European countries experienced a sharp decline in their rates of economic growth—from 10 percent rate in growth in 1960 to 3 percent lately. The logical conclusion is both striking and blunt: *the command-type planning system does not and cannot assimilate the scientific-technological revolution.* Every small technological progress requires major extra-economic effort, namely party campaigns for socialist emulation, and an enormous waste of resources and energy. The stubborn rigidity of that system has been clearly revealed by the fact that the spectacular scientific and technological breakthroughs achieved by the Soviets in the conquest of outer space and their extraordinary performances in developing most modern weapons have not made their way into the civilian production process (see Tables, 1, 2, and 3).

In recent years, a series of unprecedented critical assessments of Soviet policy has appeared in Soviet economic journals and occasionally in such important dailies as *Pravda*, *Izvestia*, and *Trud*.

In a 1982 *Pravda* article, academician V. Trapeznikov revealed the alarming fact that in 1980 the increase in Soviet national income and labor productivity was three times lower than in 1950, which means that the efficiency of investments

Table 1.
Percentages of Economic Growth in Eastern Europe

	1971-76	1976-80	1979-80	1981-85
Average annual growth rate in net material product	6.25	4.70	2.40	3.30

Source: UN Economic Commission for Europe.

Table 2.
USSR: Percentages of Average Industrial Growth

Five-Year Plans	1951-55	1956-60	1961-65	1966-70	1971-75	1976-80	1981-85
Industrial growth (average)	13.09	10.40	8.59	8.45	7.42	4.40	3.0

Source: Council of Mutual Economic Assistance bulletins, Moscow.

Table 3.
Percentage of Average Industrial Growth

	1960	1970	1980	1985
Bulgaria	15.9*	10.9*	6.0*	4.4*
Czechoslovakia	10.5	6.7	4.6	2.7
German Democratic Republic	8.7*	6.5	4.5	4.1
Poland	9.9	8.3	4.6	0.4
Romania	10.9	11.9	9.5	4.0
Hungary	7.6	6.2	3.5	1.9
USSR	10.4	8.5	4.4	3.7

*Average industrial growth of the five-year plan.

Source: Council of Mutual Economic Assistance bulletins, Moscow, 1960-86, and *Statistical Yearbook* (Moscow: Finance and Statistics Publishing House, 1981).

–capital productivity–had decreased threefold. The main cause, he pointed out, lies in the underestimation of technological scientific progress and in deficiencies in management of the national economy.[1] Indeed, in recent decades the growth of capital intensity in most socialist countries outstripped that of labor productivity, and hence capital productivity declined. *Economic Survey of Europe in 1982* made the calculations with regard to this problem (see Table 4).

Let us now see what Soviets of indisputable authority working at the Gosplan have to say in their journal *Planavoe Hozeaistvo* about the causes of the decline. In 1979, M. Gorshakov simply remarked that larger than the lag in research is "the lag in the assimilation of new technology."[2] Other Gosplan experts, L. Lnovski, V. Levedev, and S. Kuznetzov, noted that at present in the structure of metal manufacturing tools an important share is held by machine tools with manual low productivity devices.[3] Even where quantity (the forte of So-

Table 4.
Capital Productivity in Eastern Europe (Average Annual Percentage Change)

	1976	1977	1978	1979	1980	1981	1982
Bulgaria	-3.0	-1.6	-3.9	-0.3	-2.6	-2.3	1.8
Czechoslovakia	-2.1	-3.2	-1.7	-2.8	-2.8	-6.2	-6.0*
German Democratic Republic	-2.0	0.2	-2.4	-1.1	-0.8	-0.6	-4.0
Hungary	2.3	2.6	-1.1	-5.0	-6.9	-3.2	-3.0
Poland	1.7	-4.2	-5.2	-8.2	-7.0	-15.8	-9.7
Romania	-1.9	-1.5	-2.1	-3.0	-5.7	-5.8	-4.0
Soviet Union	-1.8	-2.2	-3.1	-6.4	-3.4	-3.2	-3.5*

*Calculated as the index of NMP divided by the index of fixed assets, minus 100.

Source: Calculated on the basis of the *Statisticheskii Ezhegodnik Stran Chlenov Soveta Ekonomicheskoi Vzaimopomoshchi* (CMEA statistical yearbook), 1981, 41, 49; 1982, 39, 44; and plan fulfillment reports for 1982.

viet economy) predominates, Professor S. Heinman points out that while the USSR produces more machine tools than the United States and Japan (6,552 units compared to 4,221 in the United States and 5,197 in Japan in 1977), their use in up-to-date manufacturing methods, where they can provide the highest efficiency, has not yet reached 5 percent.[4]

Soviet economists have made a series of comparative studies involving various economic phenomena as they appear in the United States and the USSR. Studying the relationship between the new industrial equipment and labor productivity, they noted that in the United States between 1948 and 1968, the rate of new industrial equipment brought into factories increased by 37.6 percent and the rate of productivity increased 200 times.[5] In the USSR, the rate of labor productivity has remained lower than that of the installation of new industrial equipment–6.3 percent for productivity and 7 percent for equipment in 1966-70, and 4.7 percent compared to 7.3 percent in 1971-78.[6]

The situation in the steel industry indicates the capacity of adaptation to technological change. In the United States between 1960 and 1974, Martin blast furnaces, considered to have become obsolete, were reduced from a share of 88.2 percent to 24.3 percent of the total steel output. Instead, new technologies (oxygen, electric arc, etc.) were introduced.[7] In the USSR, production of Martin blast furnaces continued to increase from 1960 to 1975 by 68.5 percent; as a result, in 1978 their share of total production was still 61.3 percent.[8] In other words, in the USSR enormous productive capacities based on obsolete technologies continued to be built to an extent surpassing the entire 1975 steel production of Bulgaria, Hungary, the GDR, Romania, and Czechoslovakia combined.

Technological progress by its very nature is manifest in productivity growth. Whatever the methods used to measure Soviet productivity, the conclusion has been invariably that its rate of growth compared with that of 1950-60 slows regularly to the point that it becomes negligible (see Table 5). Calcula-

Table 5.
USSR: Average Annual Rate of Growth

	1957-60	1976-70	1971-75	1976-80	1981	1982
Social labor productivity	7.75	6.8	4.6	3.2	2.6	3.2
Factory labor productivity	6.4	5.4	6	3.2	2.5	2.1

Source: Narodnoe Hozeaistvo SSSR, 1969, 1972, 1982

Table 6.
USSR: Factory Productivity-Material Sectors

1950-60	1960-70	1970-75
6.63	1.83	0.26

Source: *The Soviet Economy: Toward the Year 2000.* Abram Bergson and Herbert S. Levine, eds., (London: Allen-Unwin, 1983), 37.

tions made in the West, although somewhat reducing the figures, point in the same direction (see Table 6).

A number of economists have emphasized that the present economic mechanism inhibits technological innovations and hampers the introduction of new technology. In a 1982 article published in *Trud*, the famous constructor of airplanes Antonov revealed that managers of enterprises who decide to adopt new methods in production that were not included in the state plan are financially penalized instead of rewarded. During the June 1983 plenary session of the Central Committee of CPSU, speakers pointed out, according to *Pravda*, that "those who took risks and introduced in their activity new technologies, assimilated or produced better equipment, not infrequently found themselves at a loss, while those who shirked technical innovations were not harmed at all."[9]

Even the transfer of modern technology from the West has little effect as long as it is restricted mainly to the factory of destination. There is little effect on the other factories of the same industrial branch that continue to operate with the old technology, on the basis of which their production quotas had been set in the state plan.

Here we should recall the point made by the 1983 Novosibirsk Paper that the economic system inhibits rather than mobilizes the enormous creative power and initiative of the workers, managers, and scientists in the productive process.[10] In a system in which nothing moves unless ordered from above, workers are regarded as cogs in the economic mechanism and behave accordingly—as obediently or passively as the machines and materials—noted the author of that paper. Here is probably the crux of the problem and we shall return to it later.

Many analysts also note that as a result of the quantitative mentality and drive built into the present economic system, the disregard for the *quality* of the product has resulted in a *hypertrophy of the repair and maintenance sector*, as one economist puts it. One estimate considers the frequency of breakdown of Soviet engineering machinery at three to four times that of the United States. Indeed, Soviet statistics reveal that almost 45 percent of the nation's machine tools are engaged in the repair and maintenance sector. This sector employs more than 12 percent of the total industrial work force and accounts for approximately 25 percent of the whole metal consumption. The annual expenses for overhaul and current repairs amount to almost 40 million rubles, twice the investments in the consumer goods industries in the period 1976-80.[11] In fact, the repair sector has acquired a greater role in the reproduction of capital stock than has the construction of new machinery.

At the Twenty-seventh Congress of the CPSU, Mikhail Gorbachev directed his main criticism at the Brezhnev era for its failure to realize "the acute and urgent need for converting the economy to intensive methods of development, and for the active use in the economy of scientific and technological achievements."[12] He mentioned many cases of scientific discoveries and major inventions that failed to find practical application for years and sometimes for decades. For instance, he revealed that the development by Soviet scientists three decades ago of fundamentally new lubricants that greatly increase the service life of machine parts subjected to friction has yet to be applied on a broad scale in industry, in spite of the potential for saving many million rubles. But could such a basic shortcoming be blamed solely on "the blinkers worn by some high-ranking executives of the USSR Ministry of Petrochemical Industry and of other ministries and departments"? Why should the introduction of a new technology depend on the heads of ministries? After all, why should all decision-making power be concentrated at the top? Here is the crux of the matter.

The truth is that the more complex and diversified the national economy and the more numerous the list of items it produces, the heavier the burden of the centralized planning body. The center may be submerged under the number and complexity of problems it is supposed to solve, under the amount of information it must have in order to solve them. Newspapers in Eastern Europe are full of cases of bottlenecks in production or transportation of commodities, or of delays in delivery of goods caused by ministries or by the planning committee failing to send proper instructions on time. *Izvestia* reported one incident about a factory manager in Siberia who had been waiting more than two months to get approval from the ministry in Moscow for the replacement of a heating installation; in the meantime, 130 workers remained idle and the plan could not be fulfilled—for a loss of 3 million rubles. The manager told the paper's correspondent that he could have done the repair in 24 hours at a cost of 60,000 rubles, but he is not authorized to make such a decision.

What neither Trapeznikov nor the discussants of economic issues in recent years have properly dealt with is the socio-political side of these issues. It is this side that is now coming to the fore in the East, offering perhaps the most important explanation of the current economic downturn. I refer to the fact that the centralized and command-type planning system is one in which all the decision-making power and political initiative are concentrated at the top. If such a system could function when the country was predominantly peasant and mostly illiterate, today it cannot do so, in view of an educated multimillion working class and a huge army of competent engineers, specialists, and managers who must necessarily participate directly (and not by proxy) in both the management of the economy and the political governance of the country.

CAPITALISTS BETTER AT TECHNOLOGICAL REVOLUTION

From the beginning the Stalinist system reacted adversely to the scientific-technological revolution. In 1953, the prestigious publication *Literaturnaia Gazeta* labeled cybernetics a "science of obscurantists" and ridiculed the view that a machine can think or duplicate organic life. In October 1953 the leading Soviet philosophy journal *Voprosi Filozofi* criticized cybernetics as being opposed to dialectical materialism and denounced it as a pernicious effort by Western capitalists to extract more profits from industry by eliminating the necessity to pay wages to the proletariat. (Whom does cybernetics serve?)[13]

It was only after Stalin's death that a number of philosophers and mathematicians spoke out in favor of cybernetics. In 1961, academician Berg edited the book *Cybernetics in the Service of Communism*, in which the authors argued that no country would be able to use cybernetics as effectively as the Soviet Union. He wrote in the introduction: "In a socialist planned economy all conditions are present for the best utilization of the achievements of science and technology on behalf of all members of society rather than for various competing groups and the privileged minority" (Moscow, 1961). From then on this ideological claim—that under socialism the scientific revolution can be fully realized, in contrast to the contradictions that hinder its applications under capitalism—has become a standard judgment in Eastern literature.

However, historical experience and empirical data have shown precisely the reverse. For the last 30 years, all new major technologies have been first developed and applied on a large scale in the West. In the United States in the mid-sixties, automatic control and measurement devices and data-handling systems were used by 21,000 out of 32,000 manufacturing establishments employing over 100 persons. Nearly 9 out of 10 petroleum instrument, computer, and control equipment plants reported using these devices. Two-thirds of equipment machinery and metal working plants also were using control systems.

There is one exception to the U.S. dominance, and a very telling one. The fantastic 1957 scientific breakthrough of the Soviet Union in launching the first vehicle into outer space immediately followed by the first man, Yuri Gagarin, in space orbit dramatized Soviet superiority in mathematics and theoretical physics and its first-class educational system against the background of an economic mechanism hostile to innovation and technological change. Indeed, the only economic sector regulated by competition is the military, and there technological achievements have been spectacular.

Empirical evidence indicates that the success in the implementation of scientific and technological discoveries depends not on the nature of the socioeconomic system, whether capitalist or socialist, but on two basic conditions: (1) the level of productive forces and (2) the ability of the economic mechanism to stimulate innovation and to adapt to rapid technological change. The higher the productive forces are developed and the more mobile and flexible the economic system, the quicker the assimilation of new technologies in industry and agriculture. Of course, the motive force of the whole mechanism is competition.

The industrial societies of the West prove themselves more effective in stimulating inventions and innovations, more mobile and flexible in adapting to rapid technological change. As a result, Western capitalism has been the main beneficiary of the scientific technological revolution and the winner of the new round in the East-West economic competition. In the period 1955-80, the absolute gap between East and West in terms of per capita GNP, instead of getting closer, widened more than 1.9 times–from $4000 to $7700.[14] Comecon's share in world industrial production, which had risen in 1950-60 by 10.6 points (reaching 28.1 percent of the total), rose only 3.6 points in 1960-70 and a mere 1 point in 1970-82.[15]

Let us now see what I mean by mobility and flexibility with regard to technology. Here I must first recall Marx's theory on the concentration and centralization of capital as an objective tendency particularly strong in late capitalism. In recent decades, the concentration of capital has developed into multinational corporations. While the technological revolution has accelerated the centralization of productive forces, the same revolution has led to a business trend in the opposite direction, decentralization. It is here that capitalism has shown greater mobility.

Much has been made recently of the fact that giant corporations like General Motors and Fiat are relying more on small firms cropping up around them to produce various electric accessories or mechanical parts more cheaply and of better quality. From 1970 to 1980 most of the approximately 20 million new jobs in the United States were generated by *small* and *new* enterprises. This trend continued, even accelerated, during the recession; over the years 1981-84, long-established, large-scale manufacturing companies *lost* some 3 million jobs while businesses less than ten years old *added* at least 750,000 jobs and slightly more than a million new employees.[16]

By one count, more than one thousand new companies have started up in the Silicon Valley since 1979 and most remain small firms with fewer than 200 employees. A new breed of investors has since grown with the electronics industry. They raise $10 million to $50 million at a time to start or expand promising companies, they suggest new products and how to sell them, and they try to tempt from large corporations groups of people who are capable of forming businesses on their own.[17]

The home computer wave was begun by new and small enterprises, of which Apple (legend has it that it started in a garage) is the most famous. Steven Jobs, the founder of Apple while still in his twenties, is the man who kicked open the door to let the personal computer move into American society and who came to control a multimillion-dollar company.

The phenomenon has been called *entrepreneurship* with about one-third of it in high-technology activities and the rest in textiles and wear manufacturing, restaurant chains, and even health care units—all using *new* machinery or techniques. One specialist emphasizes that the United States has developed a unique and fairly effective system for supplying venture capital to such new enterprises. Even established companies like computer maker IBM and the giant American Telephone and Telegraph Company have begun to learn how to manage entrepreneurship within their own businesses—the so-called internal entrepreneurship. This is seen as a means to stimulate innovation in products, services, and techniques, to increase productivity, and to help companies hold on to some of their best and brightest employees. The famous clothing manufacturer Levi Strauss decided in 1982 to set aside $3 million to fund new product ideas presented by its own employees. Control Data Corporation helped some of its employees start almost eighty new businesses, among them two-year-old Global Technology Corporation specializing in computer software for training individuals in a given field or skill.[18]

Surely, such a policy *is not easy* for corporate executives accustomed to controlling everything and to making decisions at the top. "Most corporations really don't want entrepreneurs because they rip apart the warp and woof of the organization," says Professor William Zucher of the University of Pennsylvania. And yet, if a corporation wants to be innovative it must learn to manage entrepreneurs and must develop new ways for them to work within the organization.

The reason I dwell on these recent trends in the West is to put a proper perspective on the important role played by capitalists and their politics in promoting the technological revolution and its large-scale application in industry. It is fitting to recall here President Roosevelt's New Deal, the first major exercise in the economic reform of capitalist America. Under the pressure of the economic depression and internal class conflict (more than 15 million unemployed), the New Deal contributed to the economic upturn with the huge expansion of mass consumption and purchasing power of workers, implicitly by broadening the U.S. middle class as a social device to mediate class antagonisms. Although such economic policy conflicted with the reproduction needs of capital itself and with the classic scriptures of capitalist policy, thus enraging the big corporations, the New Deal opened a chapter of flexibility displayed by bourgeois leaders in sharp contrast to the rigidity and stubborn conservatism that has characterized the Soviet leadership for almost fifty years when faced with new economic and technological phenomena. We should recall here that even the modest reforms initiated by Kosygin in the sixties, relaxing a bit the heavy-handed planning system that was suffocating the initiative of workers and managers, were stubbornly resisted by the party bureaucracy and eventually rescinded by Brezhnev and his old guard associates.

Conversely, in the United States and other capitalist countries the apparatus of state monopoly was giving all possible support and encouragement to technological progress by redistributing the surplus product and by covering the losses incurred by corporations in the course of rapid technological changes.

The Novosibirsk Paper rightly points out that the basic features of the existing state system of economic management that were shaped roughly six decades ago by Stalin have never undergone a qualitative transformation to reflect basic shifts in the forces of production. For a Marxist it is almost unbelievable that a system of production relations established at a time when Russia was a backward peasant country should have been so stubbornly perpetuated in spite of the tremendous development of productive forces brought on by the technological revolution and by the immense progress in raising the level of education and the number and skill of the labor force. Thirteen million people (11.3 percent of total employment) hold university degrees and 18 million (15.7 percent of the total) have finished high schools or vocational schools, not to mention the 1.4 million Soviet scientists, a quarter of the world's scientists. We should also mention that in 1982 a full 36.8 million workers were engaged in one form or another of the vast network of evening or part-time schools. The blunt truth is that this immense human potential is very little attracted to participate in the economic decision-making process by the present highly centralized system.[19]

THE CASE OF SOVIET AGRICULTURE

Russia, at the beginning of this century, was a major grain exporting country. While most peasants were still using archaic methods, including large numbers of wooden ploughs, the large holdings were equipped with tractors and other machinery, thus providing most of the marketed production. With food consumption very low and stagnant, exports of grain in 1911-13 were 50 percent higher than in the years 1901-05.

Nature has been particularly generous with Russia, though the vast land must be viewed with mixed feelings. Large areas are taken up by Arctic and mountain regions, deserts, swamplands, and forests; nevertheless, the USSR has about 607 million hectares for agricultural needs—224 million hectares arable land, 327 million hectares pastureland, and 47 million hectares grassland. Thus, the USSR has on average 0.9 hectares of arable land per capita, which is some 23 percent more than that of the United States (0.720 hectares); with pasture, it is even better off than the U.S.: 1,256 hectares per capita compared with 0.940 hectares.

However, climatic conditions change the picture. Roughly two-thirds of all arable land in Russia is situated in the high-risk farming zone, and only one-third is in the warm zone where conditions are similar to those in the U.S. prairies. Hence, a great deal of farming in the USSR takes place in regions where winters are long and severe and where the growing season is relatively short. Therefore, ploughing, sowing, and harvesting must be carried out at the right time, neither earlier nor later.[20] Still, with modern science and technology so proficiently applied in farming these days, most of those adverse conditions could be overcome, as Canada's performance in grain output so persuasively demonstrates.

Historically, Soviet agriculture has gone through ups and downs. Immediately after the October Revolution agriculture collapsed, causing food shortages and chaos. Soviet power reacted with grain confiscations and eventually established a systematic compulsory delivery of food called *prodrazverstka*. The cumulative effect of years of low production and coercive measures caused a marked reduction in sowing, and in addition to this a severe drought hit the east and southeast, resulting in an appalling famine. The 1920 grain harvest was only half the 1909-13 average and in 1921 the harvest got even worse: 43 percent of the prewar average, 37.6 million tons.[21]

Once Lenin launched the NEP, agricultural production recovered more rapidly than industry. The grain harvest rose to 50.3 million tons in 1922 and reached 76.8 million tons in 1926.[22]

But then came the great drama of forced collectivization, initiated by Stalin like a military campaign. Grain harvest fell to 69.5 million tons in 1931, 69.9 million in 1932, 68.4 million in 1933, and 67.6 million in 1934. Livestock losses were disastrous: cattle fell from 70.5 million in 1928 to 38.4 million in 1933, pigs from 26.0 million in 1928 to 12.1 in 1933, and sheep and goats from 146.7 million to 51.9 million in the same years.[23] To cover up the disaster, Stalin invented the "biological yield" figures that were used up to his death in official statistics, inflating the real figures by some 30 million tons of grain and, in bad years (1948 and 1949) up to 50 million.

As he came to power, Khrushchev not only denounced Stalin's crimes and abuses, he also made the first frank statement on the state of Soviet agriculture. He revealed that livestock herds compared very unfavorably with 1928 and even 1916 and mentioned that butter production was lower than in czarist Russia. The distortion of grain crop figures, had been so blatant that for a while grain statistics were kept secret. Khrushchev took a series of measures designed to ease the coercion and to stimulate agricultural output. Compulsory-procurement prices and over-quota delivery prices were increased, past debts of kolkhozes to the state were written off, private plots were freed of all compulsory delivery obligations, and so on. He then launched his program for a spectacular expansion of cultivated land. As a result, total grain harvest rose from 82.5 million tons in 1953 to 134.7 million in 1958, while the number of animals rose but at a slower pace.[24]

Khrushchev's erratic behavior was then reflected in the inflated seven-year plan of 1958-65, the results of which were very disappointing. Instead of the ambitious 70 percent increase, total agricultural output rose only by 14 percent.

During the Brezhnev era the volume of investment in agriculture soared beyond precedent: 69 percent of total investments earmarked for agriculture and industries supplying and servicing the agricultural sector. This resulted in a significant increase in output approaching 200 million tons of grain annually by 1980 but stopped at that level for a number of years still far from the 260 million ton level considered a must by Soviet economists in order to cover both the consumption of the population and the needs in fodder if animal growth was to proceed according to the plan. Actually, with six poor harvests in a row (1979-1984) the USSR has been compelled to import between 40 and 50 million tons of grain annually.

In summary, Soviet agricultural growth has not kept pace either with urban population growth or with the increasing demand generated by rising wages and standard of living; productivity in grain output and lifestock remains much lower than that in the West and even than that in Eastern Europe.

This is not the place, nor is this writer qualified, to pinpoint the causes of the serious failure of the Soviet system. That 70 years after the Revolution the second greatest world power cannot feed its people and must import each year from capitalist countries tens of millions of tons of grain and large quantities of meat and butter is something that touches the very heart of socialism's raison d'etre.

Hundreds of studies have been devoted to Soviet agriculture. Leaving aside those that are ideologically biased, most authors emphasize three main causes of the problem: (1) the neglect of the agricultural sector during the Stalin era; (2) the over-centralized planning and management of Soviet agriculture; and (3) the inability of Soviet industry to supply the inputs required by agriculture in machinery, chemicals, and so on. Probably an exhaustive analysis should consider each of these three points but since Stalin's era is many decades behind us and the attention given by his successors to the problems of agriculture has increased over time, particularly in investment policy, I am inclined to insist mainly on the second item. Here I would put a special emphasis on the lack of understanding shown by the Soviet leadership of the very nature of farming, that which makes it different from the other sectors of the economy. I refer to the fact that those who farm must exercise the kind of initiative and performance that, to a greater extent than in industry, cannot be controlled or supervised. With farm workers engaged in a series of operations to be stubbornly followed over months and even years from beginning to end, being compelled most of the time to adapt performance to particular circumstances (e.g., weather conditions) that cannot be always anticipated, the emphasis falls on the individual motivation of the peasant to work hard and well, namely to do a "smart work". The individual farm worker who carefully grows vegetables and fruits, who painstakingly takes care of cattle, pigs, or chickens, and who is interested in harvesting quickly and depositing the grains safely—that is the decisive factor in agriculture.

Much more than in industry, *initiative* is an essential ingredient in farming. Only a cooperative that organizes, manages, and stimulates the farmer to do a good job can pave the way toward socialism in agriculture. The excessive talk about collectivism in the countryside is perhaps the most salient expression of the Soviet misconception of what agriculture is all about.

Lenin was aware of this specific feature of agriculture when he pointed out that socialism must be preceded by a cultural revolution in the village and that the peasant should be brought to socialism through cooperatives based on marketing, buying, and credit. Instead, Stalin resorted to administrative means and coercion, creating a system of planning and management from above in which the decisive factor simply does not exist. This is not to say that other factors (land, investment, education, management versus mismanagement, weather conditions) do not count in agriculture. My point is that the effectiveness of the other factors can be significantly enhanced or diminished by the way the farm worker's initiative and role is handled.

Let us illustrate this point with investments. I have already mentioned the fabulous increase of investments in agriculture since 1965. Yet, during the period 1965-80 the capital intensity of agriculture has moved upwards very little. Brezhnev in 1980 admitted that "in entire regions investments increase but production over a number of years stands pat."[25] On average, for every 1 percent increase in productive fixed assets during the seventies, the volume of gross agricultural output increased by only 0.74 percent; moreover, the figures show that increasing investment resources have to be applied in order to keep agricultural output increasing at a constant rate. The volume of output produced per ruble of fixed assets has fallen sharply from approximately 82 kopecs of gross output per ruble in 1961-65 to 78 kopecs in 1966-70 to 58 kopecs in 1971-75. An enormous quantity of resources is being poured into agriculture for a relatively meager return.[26]

Nothing reveals more strikingly the behavior of the Soviet farmer in this context than the evolution of labor productivity. Whereas in the West over the past ten to fifteen years productivity increased by 2.5 percent for every 1 percent increase of agricultural labor output, in the USSR productivity increased by an average of only 1.03 percent in 1961-65, 1.07 percent in 1966-70, and 1.65 percent in 1971-75.[27] Actually, despite the increasingly enormous investments, the rate of growth of farm labor output declined precisely because of the decline of productivity. Even compared with Hungary (41.69 quintals) and Bulgaria (35.49 quintals) the average grain production per hectare in the USSR in 1976-80 was much lower: 16.0 quintals.

We should mention here that the annual level of deliveries of machinery, equipment, and industrial materials (e.g., fertilizers and fuel) was 50 percent higher in 1970-79, which forces upon us the conclusion that it is the farm worker's poor performance that chiefly determined the decline in productivity growth.

TURBULENCE AND DEVIANCE IN EASTERN EUROPE

To better understand political and economic developments in Eastern Europe, we must go back to the origins of the modern international system. It was the vigorous expansion of capitalism and the formation of nation-states that gave the Western half of Europe a strong edge over the Eastern half. The Renaissance, with its merging of classical antiquity and late feudalism, together with its path-breaking scientific discoveries, marks the historical point at which Europe began to outdistance the other continents. And since the Renaissance was a West European phenomenon par excellence, it was *there* that the core of the international system was established. This Western predominance was reinforced by the Industrial Revolution, allowing Western powers to expand capitalism and to acquire vast colonial empires; an international division of labor was set up between capitalism in the West and the peripheral regions in Africa, Asia, and Latin America. In the process, the West became highly industrialized and rich, while the periphery remained underdeveloped and poor.

In Eastern Europe, peoples and nationalities–most still struggling for nationhood–remained largely agricultural with strong feudal structures lasting until the twentieth century. Such were the historical conditions that explain why later the East-West conflict would contain strong features of the North-South antagonism.

Political developments after World War II in Europe can be divided into two historical periods. The first, beginning with 1945 and extending until the end of the fifties, was dominated by the division of Europe along ideological lines into two opposite and hostile camps tightly lined up behind the United States and the USSR. It was the extension into Eastern Europe of the revolutionary process under the Soviet military umbrella that led the United States and its Western allies to counter with such measures as the containment policy, the North Atlantic Treaty Organization, the Marshall Plan, and the Truman Doctrine. *Class conflict and the ideology that goes with it* were pushed to the forefront of world politics. The Cold War was the virulent expression of that priority in international affairs.

The second historical development after World War II began with the halting of the wind of change in Europe at the end of the fifties, when the thrust of revolution shifted toward the underdeveloped continents and the Third World began looking for a place in the sun. National resurgence permeated world politics. In the West, General de Gaulle came out against U.S. domination, in the East the Sino-Soviet polemics broke out. Against this background the United States and the USSR discovered their common interest in maintaining their nuclear strategic lead. The two nuclear treaties (test ban and nonproliferation) jointly drafted by Soviet and American experts reflect this common policy. In short, a new stage opened up in world politics in which *national-strategic* considerations would override ideological ones.

Implied in this analysis are two theoretical assumptions: It is the aggregation of people according to *class* interests or *ethnic* ties that conditions their behavior and thinking whenever they engage collectively in large-scale movements. As one or the other motive force expands on a sufficiently large international scale, it may well become predominant in the entire international system. Hence, modern history, beginning with the French Revolution, has been marked by periods of intense national competition alternating with periods of sharp class-ideological conflict. I call this historical interplay the seesaw of class and national motive force in international politics, for as one comes to prevail the other begins to lose its impact on foreign policies.

My contention is that during the two periods of postwar Europe, the relations between the superpowers with their partners in Western and Eastern Europe bear a certain resemblance. Major political developments in both parts of Europe, though different internally because of their socioeconomic systems, have displayed striking similarities. During the Cold War, both Western and Eastern nations were tightly aligned behind their respective leaders. The position of the United States and the USSR was similar: undisputed authority, monopoly in the formulation of policy and strategy, complete subordination to the goals set in Washington and Moscow. As national-strategic issues prevailed over ideology in both East and West, nations gaining strength within both alliances began to assert themselves and promote national interests, gradually demanding a voice in the formulation of policies and military doctrines. In the West, France led the way toward political emancipation, followed by West Germany's Ostpolitik. In the East the trend is reflected in such events as those in Hungary and Poland in 1956, later in Romania's independent stance, and last but not least in Czechoslovakia. To be sure, the phenomenon is stronger in Western Europe, where the asymmetric structure of the alliance is less overwhelming than that in the

East, where the Soviet Union's power exceeds by far that of all its allies together. Also, the social content of national self-assertion in the East is different from that in the West. What has been wrongly called in the Western literature "liberalization" is actually the attempt of local revolutionary forces to *remake socialism in their own way*, according to national and political tradition. We must recall that in the aftermath of World War II the Soviet Union was the dominant power in the region, enjoying the glory of liberator from Nazi oppression. To both the Soviet Communist party and the local Communist parties of Eastern Europe the mechanical adoption of the Soviet model seemed the best and safest course, particularly in view of the vigorous assault of the imperialist powers seeking to disrupt and destabilize by subversion and sabotage the infant political regimes. Whereas in the Cold War period international conditions were conducive to subordination within the bloc and to close imitation of the Soviet model, now international conditions favor the reverse trend—that is, self-assertion of national revolutionary forces, emphasis on national equality and cultural identity, and rejection of forms and methods in building socialism that are ill-suited to the given nation. In Romania, where servile mimicry had gone as far as declaring Romanian language and culture as chiefly Slavic, the country's Latin heritage was restored to recognition. The Prague Spring in Czechoslovakia was essentially a drive to remake socialism consistent with national conditions. Czechoslovakia had been even before the revolution an industrial state with a high level of culture and a tradition of political democracy. It was actually the only Eastern country that was ripe for socialism, according to Marx's paradigm. Surely, such a nation could hardly assimilate the Soviet model which had been tailored in a backward country.

Now, if we only translate some of the notions used in the East into Western terms and consider the whole process within a capitalist milieu, we shall easily discover the resemblance.

Change USSR to United States, and you will have in the West: a trend toward national emancipation, increasing insistence on participation in the making of NATO strategy, and promotion of an independent trade and monetary policy coming into conflict with U.S. supremacy. While nationalism had bad connotations to both Washington and Moscow, the moment it was monitored in the rival camp the pejorative adjectives were suddenly replaced by terms of praise and encouragement. De Gaulle was scorned in Washington and praised in Moscow; and so was Romania in reverse.

This is not to say that class interests have vanished altogether in the making of foreign policy. Even de Gaulle, when he perceived the Cuban missile crisis as a test of power with an underlying ideological component, immediately assured President Kennedy of France's support. Also, while pulling French troops out of NATO, France remained in the Atlantic alliance because de Gaulle realized that capitalism could not be maintained by France alone. Class interests and the ideology that goes with them have remained to this day the cement that keeps NATO members together.

Originating in the clashing ideological climate of the Cold War, NATO and the Warsaw Treaty have survived the centrifugal forces of nationalism through a stabilizing system that is feeding its own dynamics as the institutional framework of the bipolar structure of power in Europe. At the heart of this system lies the mutual distrust inherited from the Cold War which is continually reinforced by the mutual fear that any lowering of the guard may pose a challenge to the very bases of society as they exist in both West and East.

Thus, military pacts with an ideological underpinning have two major functions: one, openly proclaimed, is directed outward; the other, well disguised, is directed inward. The former is meant to protect pact members against an external threat; the latter, to secure the perpetuation of the system of relations inside the alliance, its structure of power. Between the two functions, a self-adjustment mechanism is at work. When the external threat of aggression is imminent, the outward function takes precedence while the inward one recedes into the background. When the external threat diminishes, the inward function prevails. If need be, the military pact is used to restore order inside—that is, to deal with challenges to the system. The external threat is then only a pretext of a cover-up for the internal operation. Dubcek with his Prague Spring simply ignored the second function of the Warsaw Treaty and so did the leadership of Solidarity in Poland. In the West, Kissinger's warnings against Communist participation in Italy's government (described as a threat to NATO), and later U.S. public displeasure with Mitterand's decision to bring three Communist ministers into his cabinet fall within the same conception of NATO's dual role: safeguarding the capitalist system inside is no less important than repelling the external aggression.

The relations between NATO and the Warsaw Pact constitute the matrix of the worldwide war system. As a result, the arms race has been kept on an ascending line in Europe, regardless of the fluctuations in the political climate or whether the spirit of detente has prevailed or subsided. Direct military expenditures in both NATO and the Warsaw Pact have kept rising unperturbed by the Nixon-Brezhnev accord on detente, SALT I and II, the quadripartite agreement on West Berlin, Ostpolitik, and the Helsinki Conference on European Security and Cooperation. There is but one conclusion: The war system, originating in the competitive nature of the international interstate system, works no matter the political climate or the socioeconomic system.

Turbulence in Poland

As each month passes in Poland, the problems confronting the Communist party appear ever more complex and consequently more difficult to solve. It seems that the social explosion that began during the hot summer of 1980 in the coastal city of Gdansk has triggered a process of change involving not only the economy but the very core of the political system as well.

That such a fundamental challenge would eventually have to be faced was already obvious to anyone who studied carefully the historic document signed on 31 August 1980 by the leaders of the "new, independent and self-governing trade unions" and the representative of the Polish government. Indeed, the twenty-one demands accepted by the government dealt not only with working conditions, substantial wage increases, the right to strike, higher pensions, better food supplies, hospitals, housing, and the five-day work week, but also with the end of censorship, freedom of expression and religion, release of political prisoners, and trade union participation in economic reform and policy.

Surely, an unbiased observer would cry: But these are socialist goals and could be easily found in the Manifesto and other documents drafted by Karl Marx for the working classes more than a century ago! What is more, that the struggle for such demands and goals should break out from below, from the masses, should not strike a Marxist as something unusual or alien to socialist ideology. After all, the great revolutionary advances in human history have always come from the toiling masses. This is precisely what makes recent political developments in Poland so difficult to manage and explain.

The case of Poland is particularly significant. Although in the early 1970s, chiefly on the basis of foreign loans and credits, investment in industry was so huge that Poland jumped to tenth place among industrial nations, the inability to export toward the end of the decade (because of the world economic crisis), coupled with the total neglect of agriculture and consumer goods, brought the Polish economy to the verge of bankruptcy. With foreign debt soaring toward $24 billion, Poland had to pay $6 billion a year merely on debt servicing at a time when the government had to spend millions of extra dollars on food imports. To lesser extent, all East European countries are indebted to Western banks and pay high annual interest rates.

Although in Czechoslovakia the initiative for change in 1968 came from a section of the top leadership, in Poland we have witnessed an explosion from below that is more difficult to control internally and is counterproductive to suppress from outside. In Prague it was Dubcek and the new Politburo who led, according to the vision of "socialism with a human face," the program of economic and political democratization. In Poland it is the working class that is pushing for change, with the Communist party fighting a rearguard action and at the same time struggling to formulate a program of "renewal" under pressure from below.

To assess correctly the significance and potential impact of events in Poland on Eastern Europe as a whole, we must distinguish between the common problems already discussed and the peculiar features of Poland itself. The most important peculiarities are probably these powerful influences: the role of the Roman Catholic church (even stronger among workers than in Italy) and the century-long tradition of popular struggles and uprisings in the name of freedom, independence, and various social causes. These are part of the Polish character, and social eruptions have not been uncommon since the end of World War II, with the prolonged strike of 1980 marking a transition from spontaneity to organization, from sporadic local battles to the emergence of Solidarity as a national group encompassing the overwhelming majority of the working class.

As far as Catholicism is concerned, it is now stronger than before World War II; we should bear in mind that the perversion of socialist ideology that has accompanied the pursuit of capital accumulation by the state has greatly contributed to religious revival. Lenin used to say that there was no such thing as an ideological vacuum; as one ideology loses ground in the popular consciousness it is necessarily replaced by an alternative. If Lech Walesa, the leader of the workers' movement, had not been a Catholic before, the sight of militia ordered by the leadership to shoot people protesting price increases shortly before Christmas would have made him one, particularly since he was fired from his job for joining the protest.

Hence, the Communist party, led by Stanislaw Kania, was struggling to save its own "leading role" under adverse conditions. Industrial output was falling, and the mining of coal, Poland's main currency-earning export, was lagging while continual skirmishes between the new unions and the authorities maintained a tension that negatively affected the working of the entire economy.

The situation in agriculture was equally bad. With 3.5 million privately owned farms covering 75 percent of the available arable land and producing 80 percent of the nation's food, the government was hardly in a position to improve agricultural output unless it came to terms with the peasants and produced a crash program to help them with credits, machinery, and strong material incentives in the food market. Thirty years of neglect were striking back with a vengeance.

Military rule in Poland appeared as the last resort once it became obvious that the governing body of the Communist party could no longer win the allegiance of society by economic and ideological means. Indeed, we could hardly find in European history examples of a political regime more bereft of social support. The Communist government, mired in economic sluggishness and stripped of its only legitimacy—the ideological claim of embodying the interests of the working class—watched impotently as ever wider sections of society organized against it.

The military at least came in with a clean slate. It could argue that it saved the country from foreign occupation or from a bloody civil war, a point most Poles would probably agree with, however much they dislike martial law. Nonetheless, the military has been waging a "limited war" with harsh repressive measures, massive internments in camps, and violent clashes in Gdansk, Katowice, and Poznan.

How could this happen in Eastern Europe, defying the most sacred tenets of the system? And how much can one play around with ideology just for the sake of holding on to power?

From the very beginning, Poland's powerful movement for social change wrestled with the critical question: How far can we go? It is a question that must be answered before it is too late by every revolutionary movement in the neighborhood of the two giants of our time, whether in Cuba, Nicaragua, or San Salvador, or in Hungary, Czechoslovakia, or Poland. As the old saying goes, when you're in bed with an elephant, you'd better watch out which way he turns. Apparently the leaders of Solidarity tragically neglected this warning and failed to grasp the hard fact that the Polish state is embedded in a regional structure of power buttressed by the Warsaw Pact militarily and by the Council for Mutual Economic Assistance economically.

There were five major actors, both foreign and domestic, involved in the Polish crisis—the USSR, the Catholic church, the Western banks, Solidarity, and the Communist party. With five contending players, one could not cross the limits defined by the others without precipitating a showdown. The rule of the game, therefore, was self-restraint.

As the product of an explosive movement, Solidarity experienced the greatest difficulties in obeying that rule. What's more, the new unions had no unifying ideology other than an almost wild reaction against all that had been presented as "socialism" or "Marxism-Leninism" by an unscrupulous leadership. Even Solidarity's demand for workers' self-management—so manifest a goal of socialism—was never acknowledged as such in order to avoid any reference to the regime's cynical distortion of socialist principles.

But because it lacked a unified ideological creed, Solidarity was at the mercy of various influences and manipulations.

Local unions called strikes for whatever reasons, while the national leaders clashed over the best tactics to achieve something that was never clearly defined. Small wonder that the initial trade union grievances quickly gave way to ever more ambitious political aims.

The West noisily encouraged this trend, although such political demands of unions have never been acceded to there. As for the Vatican, the standards for Poland seem to be totally different from those applied in Latin America, where Pope John Paul II has been trying hard to keep priests out of political movements.

In retrospect, Lech Walesa seems to have had a better sense of the limits of the movement. Kuron, founder of the opposition group KOR (Committee of Workers Defense) and theoretician of Solidarity, was the only one who defined the limits: Do not challenge the Communist party's dominance over the central administration, the police forces, and the army—that is, the institutional setting of the power structure—while struggling for autonomy in every other sphere of life with the focus on local power. Such a strategy could easily go along with the economic reform providing for decentralization and self-management, which explains why Walesa approved it. But each time he tried to chart such a sensible course for Solidarity, he was overruled by the kind of anarchic militants who easily make it to the top in such a movement.

As for the Communist party, the conservative hard-liners frustrated every attempt of Kania, and then Jaruzelski, to reach a modus vivendi with Solidarity. At the same time they conducted a fierce struggle against the advocates of renewal, a struggle that had been paralyzing the leadership ever since the party Congress. The fact that the conservative "forums" Katowice and Poznan were praised by the Soviet press as "true Marxist-Leninists" gave a clear signal of Moscow's choice.

Then, under martial law, the hard-liners and the orthodox party functionaries who earlier retreated into the shadows for fear of being identified with the Gierek administration were becoming increasingly aggressive and articulate. And yet the system had been fatally wounded in both its economic and political flanks. Jaruzelski and his associates knew very well that a return to the pre-Gdansk agreement in Poland would be inconceivable.

The leadership, facing an unprecedented drop of almost 15 percent in industrial output, an agriculture in complete disarray, and a growing foreign debt, proclaimed economic reform as the most urgent item in the renewal program as early as the winter of 1980. Even after Walesa agreed with the draft of a law outlining a Hungarian type of economic reform, however, the Central Committee failed to adopt it in plenary meeting or in parliament. Why?

The trouble is that such a deep economic reform involves not only the structure of prices, the wage system, and management of enterprises, but also the whole conception of central planning and decision making concentrated at the top—and here things stopped.

Of course, Poland is not Hungary. Moreover, the relaxation measures announced by the military so quickly followed by the resurgence of Solidarity's fighting force have all but shown that normalization of the Czechoslovak type will not work in Poland. Hence, the only positive alternative is a sort of social understanding between the Communist party and Solidarity with the backing of the church. This time international conditions may favor such a gambit, for right now Moscow's overriding objective in Eastern Europe is stability. If a Polish domestic arrangement could promise to keep the turmoil under control, previous objections will probably subside. The question is whether such an arrangement between the Communist party and Solidarity could succeed at a time when each feels disabled and frustrated because of the other.

Deviance in the East

When someone in the Kremlin sneezes, the Bulgarians get the flu, says a rather widespread joke. Another stereotype depicts East Germany as exceedingly conformist. And, of course, everybody knows that Hungary is a most faithful supporter of Soviet foreign policy. And yet, a Soviet or Romanian visitor who steps into the shopping centers and markets of Sofia, Berlin, or Budapest will be struck by the variety of consumer goods and foodstuffs, not to mention the attractive presentation. Probably the view of food stores without the familiar lines along the sidewalks will strike the visitor most, causing wonderment about where he or she is.

In Sofia, the girl in the bakery wears a neat white apron and uses special metal tongs to serve rolls and bread: A nationwide campaign for cleanliness is going on in Bulgaria. Customers are asked to behave and not to touch fruits, meat, or vegetables. Why, thinks the visitor, are such things available and such time and energy devoted to please the consumer? In Berlin one finds three kinds of milk, and in Budapest the section in the department store selling chicken, geese, and turkeys is separated from that selling beef, pork, and liver.

Are these nations rightist or leftist deviationists? the visitor will finally ask. In fact, all three nations, although very orthodox ideologically, have deviated in different ways and degrees from the Stalinist economic model—by which I mean a model based on four major principles: (1) priorities for heavy industry to the detriment of consumer goods industries and agriculture; (2) command-type planning of every sector of the economy; (3) strict centralization of decision making; and (4) emphasis on administrative means in running the economy. Stalin, aware that ideology is the main indispensable instrument for legitimizing power systems, proceeded to mold socialist ideology according to his economic system. That Stalinism has been so fervently appropriated by the party apparat and turned into ideological dogma seems quite natural: Central planning of the economy and administration offers the party apparat the best way to acquire and consolidate power. We are thus dealing with a symbiosis of economic policy and power that explains both the strength and resilience of Stalinism long after the death of its maker. And, as Poland shows, the apparat will stop at nothing to perpetuate its power.

Hungary Sets the Pace

As I drove toward Budapest in 1982 my first impression was that the villages along the modern highway looked more prosperous than those of the eastern part of Austria. In front of their pretty houses peasants were displaying a great variety of fresh fruits and vegetables. Next morning, as I made my way to the covered market in Dimitrov Square, I noticed that the huge hall was equally divided: on the left were the state shops, well supplied with every basic food item; on the right, individual stalls belonging to peasants with a colorful display of special vegetables and herbs and a wide selection of fresh meat (especially pork and veal), smoked hams, paprika-flavored *gyula* sausages, homemade pies, and lots of cheeses. Competition was fierce and business brisk as I watched the peasant women with their black kerchiefs and vividly colored blouses, loudly calling the customers and driving a hard bargain with each of them.

Foreign observers call this a "quiet revolution." The *Wall Street Journal* headlines its report from Budapest: "Hungary tries a bit of capitalism," and *Die Presse* of Vienna exclaims: "Eastern Europe discovers private initiative." To be eclectic I will say that there is some truth in each of these statements. As a whole, however, the Hungarian model is neither a return to capitalism nor what is called market socialism. It is essentially an updated Leninist NEP, conceived this time not merely as a tactical strategem to revive an agonizing economy but as a long-term strategy for the industrialization and modernization of a less-developed country with a view of reaching real socialism. Thus, the economic system is mixed with the plan regulating the macroeconomic level and the market regulating agriculture and consumer goods industries. This arrangement is scientifically based on the assumption that the plan is effective in running the production of capital goods; in agriculture and consumer goods industries, where the law of value regulates production and distribution, the plan is ineffective if it uses the administrative method in managing these economic sectors. The socialist state cannot disregard the economic laws operating here except at the risk of failure—chronic shortages of food, shabby consumer goods, and poor services. Illustrations are abundant in the East wherever the Stalinist model is still in place.

It all began with the historic party resolution of 7 May 1966, ten years after the social earthquake that shook Hungary: "The development of an active role for the market requires the cumbersome and bureaucratic state system of the centralized allocation of materials and products to give place to commercial relations, i.e., producers should be able to decide within their range of activities what and how much they produce and offer for sale, as well as from whom they purchase the necessary inputs." The wording sounded revolutionary, but the implementation was gradual and prudent.

To do away with the old anachronistic system, the government began by relaxing its control over individual enterprises; local managers were given a greater say in investment, production, and price decisions, while the state retained overall control through credit, price, wage, and foreign trade "regulators." But the conservative forces with their old habits reacted strongly against the so-called restoration of capitalism.

Interestingly, the managers and workers in inefficient factories joined the hard-liners of the party apparat to save their threatened jobs; as a result, some of the measures were rescinded and central control was tightened again. But the world economic crisis and the steep rise of prices for oil and other raw materials brought Hungary to the brink of disaster. The leadership then decided to go ahead with the reform in a resolute manner, cracking down on the hard-liners.

A radical revision of the price structure, however painful, proved to be the centerpiece of the economic reform. For without eliminating state subsidies and other artificial elements that distort the economic process, and without bringing prices closer to the real cost of the product, one cannot evaluate the actual performance of the economic units and of the economy as a whole. In 1979, prices of basic foodstuffs were raised 20 percent. But since the subsidies on meat, milk, cereals, and so on had been much higher, the government kept adjusting prices, until lately. In 1980, about 60 percent of industrial goods were priced according to the world market. The idea behind this policy was simple: Producer prices should accurately reflect true economic costs.

The success of the economic reform has been particularly evident in agriculture. Hungary is now one of the most efficient world food producers: In per capita output it is second to the United States in corn, third to Canada and Australia in wheat, and a close second to Denmark in pork. The key to this success is to be found in the elimination of the heavy-handed planning system that suffocated agriculture and in the creation of an ingenious relationship between the large socialist cooperatives and the private plots of farmers essentially based on material incentives. The cooperatives are providing their members who want to tend private plots with land (up to 6,000 square meters), fodder, seeds, fertilizers, agronomic advice, and veterinary assistance; chickens, rabbits, and pigs are given to private households on a contractual basis.

This organically links the households to the cooperative, which remains dominant.

I visited a cooperative near Budapest, the vice president of which is in charge of the coordination of private plot activities of members of the co-op after working hours. Last year the average monthly income of the co-op member was just over 3,500 forints compared with the average industrial wage of 3,700 forints per worker.

Because life is much cheaper in the village, Hungary is the only Eastern country with a migration in reverse: from city to countryside. Just by growing a plot of raspberries, a worker can double his or her income, though this requires hard work well after dark. Hence, about 4 million people are tending private plots: 80,000 are members of cooperatives, 1,100,000 have jobs in industry, and 1,200,000 are pensioners. In 1980 they devoted 2.3 billion hours of work and contributed a 30 to 35 percent share of the gross agricultural product, worth more than 60 billion forints.

Equally interesting is the division of labor in agriculture. The cooperatives specialize in grain production, which is much more efficient in large-scale farming, and the household producers concentrate on produce that is labor-intensive and requires painstaking care: vegetables and fruits, poultry, rabbits, pigs, and cattle.

Over time the popular perception of this activity also has changed. Initially, household plots were viewed as a means to enrich the ever-greedy peasants; today they enjoy the appreciation of the workers for the fine quality and reliability of their products.

The average size of the household plot is rather small but it is cultivated intensively. Istvan Szendrei, in his late 50s, is a member of the nearby Bocskai Cooperative. He and his wife earn about one-third of their income from raising 75 to 85 pigs per year and cultivating poppies.

Imre Vince belongs to the younger generation and is more aggressive. He produces independently 500 to 600 pigs per year in a backyard of about 4000 square meters, buying fodder from the cooperative. He and his family, working together, can afford many luxuries, including two compact cars. With such high productivity, it is small wonder that household plots and private farmers account for more than half of the output of pigs, poultry, and fruits in Hungary.

As for small business, Hungarian economists have been arguing that even in highly industrialized countries dominated by monopolies, thousands of small firms employing few workers can flourish alongside such giants as General Motors and Fiat. The reason is simple. Items like bulbs or screws can be produced more cheaply by specialized small enterprises. Therefore, Hungary decided to reverse the Stalinist trend toward industrial gigantism and to break up some large enterprises into smaller ones that produce small parts and accessories, obtain the waste materials and tools of the enterprise, or undertake repair and maintenance services. Thus, an extensive system of useful auxiliary activities has taken shape in industry and services. Today, only 25 percent of consumer services are performed by socialist enterprises; the rest are provided by private workshops with the result that services have significantly improved, productivity has risen, and prices have declined because of competition. The fact is that such things as repair of an apartment, of plumbing, or of the television set, which used to be an almost impossible undertaking, are now easy to get—and cheaper.

Recently, a new experiment was encouraged in the retail trade: the Skala Co-op, a sixty-six-store group that overtook the government-owned Centrum chain to become Hungary's largest retail organization. Skala is supposed to launch a competitive challenge to dreary state-owned department stores by going straight to the producers, setting up its own wholesale organization, arranging exclusive contracts with some factories, exchanging items with department stores in other socialist countries, and eventually negotiating arrangements with West European suppliers. Employees receive a premium based on performance but are fired if they don't want to work. The first Skala department store has already recorded twice the average sales of its state competitors of the same size. The owners of Skala are two hundred consumer cooperatives that have invested money in the group to get a share of the annual profits according to the size of their investment.

Hungary is far from having solved all its economic problems. It struggles fiercely with its foreign debt, with the inevitable hitches resulting from such a radical overhaul, and with the negative effects of the world crises burdening every country with few natural resources. But there is a feeling of participation among the masses, both urban and rural, and a candid dialogue between the leaders and the working people that is almost unique in Eastern Europe. Every month there is a "Party Day" when members of the Central Committee come to the factories, not to make speeches but to answer questions and discuss with the workers all decisions bound to affect them.

A law enacted in 1978 gave the workers the right to veto management decisions and established the principle of workers' direct participation in the management of enterprises through their local union. As a rule, every major decision of the manager regarding work organization, wages and bonuses, investments, introduction of new technology, contracts with other enterprises, and the like may be taken only in consultation with the factory committee representing the workers.

At the national level, the president of the unions and his associates meet twice a year with the prime minister to discuss major decisions of economic policy, once at the headquarters of the unions and once in the cabinet of the prime minister. A detailed report on the issues that have been discussed, the positions and arguments of each party, and the agreement eventually reached is then published the next day in the press.

In 1979, when the government was preparing a drastic restructuring of food prices, the unions countered with the proposal of a 20 percent raise in wages, which in turn required the government to cut some investments. This procedure may well explain why the painful increases in food prices were accepted by the workers.

Thus, a gradual process of democratization—kept well under control, to be sure—is taking place as a result of the economic restructuring. Typical in this respect is the popular TV program "66," moderated by Janos Ban, in which members of the government are called to account for their activities or decisions, having to answer questions coming from 66 citizens who are regularly invited on the air to grill top officials about domestic issues. Guest officials are first questioned by the moderator and later by members of the audiences selected on the basis of their letters of complaint. In both cases, the audience pushes buttons to vote on whether the answer is satisfactory or not; in the latter case the dignitary is given a chance to offer further argument or change the position. Another TV entry, "Windows," invites consumer complaints about products and government services and then investigates them. Thus, television is airing popular concerns and divergent views to an extent unthinkable in other Eastern countries.

Bulgaria: A Maverick?

Bulgaria, in the 1950s, gave priority to agriculture in investment policy; only after modernizing did it switch to heavy industry. This rational policy may well explain why Bulgaria, the poorest of the lot, has made the most spectacular advance in Eastern Europe, jumping from a prewar $250 per capita GNP to well over $3,000 in 1980. The share of industry in the national income is now about 60 percent; but this does not prevent Bulgaria from being the major world producer of judo equipment and to play host right in the center of Sofia to two elegant boutiques of Pierre Cardin, the French fashion designer—one for women, the other for men—a unique display in the East. In the famous Black Sea resort of Varna, Bulgarian architects have built attractive one-family cottages along the beach; the idea was that urban people fed up with living in huge apartment buildings would prefer a cottage for the holidays. That they do is not surprising, but that an Eastern government went along with such an idea is.

You see how wrong a joke like the one with the Kremlin's sneeze and the Bulgarian flu can be. One wishes the reverse were true.

What is more, as the steep rise of oil prices and other effects of the world economic crisis began to take their toll, Bulgaria decided to reduce the role of central planning. In 1979, the government introduced quasi-market relationships, beginning with agriculture and extending the so-called new economic mechanism to branches of consumer goods industries. To encourage the output of high-demand products on the home and foreign markets, bonuses are offered in excess of state prices, agricultural prices are systematically adjusted to the market demand, and cooperatives are no longer taxed according to their income but to the amount and quality of their land so that the more efficient ones can get a higher surplus for wages and investment. As a result, Bulgaria together with Hungary are the only East European countries with a significant surplus for export in their agricultural balance of trade.

In Bulgaria also a significant percentage (27 to 28 percent) of total farm output is from private plots; a Bulgarian peasant may cultivate about 10 acres and may use an additional 3.7 acres of pasture. The peasant gets fodder, fertilizers, and the use of machines from the state and repays with farm produce.

It is interesting that in Bulgaria there is also a fierce struggle, though muted by ideological restrictions, between the advocates of extending market relations and the bureaucrats clinging to central planning. At the 1980 Central Committee plenum, conservative forces in the party apparat were warned that they must comply with the new economic mechanism or face "resolute countermeasures by the party and the state." Indeed, Prime Minister Stanco Todorof was soon demoted.

The record of the new economic mechanism speaks for itself. Bulgarian agriculture has achieved in recent years an annual increase of 10 percent in overall output and 29 percent in grains. In 1982, Bulgaria produced one ton of grain per capita. Such startling results have enabled the government to set up in every major factory special food stores called *gastronom* and a great variety of small workshops for services within the precinct of the factory. In the morning, before going to the workplace, the workers place their orders in the food store, including meat, and after work they pick up their purchases, pay the bill, and go home—all without having to stand for hours in line, sometimes without getting what they wanted, as so often happens in other socialist countries. Thirty-two hundred such *gastronom* stores and 1,400 small workshops already function as annexes of Bulgarian factories.

But my greatest surprise came when I discovered that Bulgaria is now one of the most advanced nations in Eastern Europe in modern technology, being the first to introduce Japanese robots and microprocessors. By 1985, a third of operations in the machine tool industry was performed by equipment and numerical command. The manager of the electrical plant Electra told us that none of his products remains in production more than three years. I was then reminded of a recent article in the Soviet newspaper *Trud* in which the famous Soviet aircraft designer Antonov revealed that the present planning system in effect rewards inefficient production and penalizes factories that try to improve quality or introduce new technology.

The Secret of the German Democratic Republic

Berlin is the capital of the tenth-leading industrial state in the world. Steel mills and citadels of the machine tool industry preside over the economic life of the city as symbols of socialist power. But here and there one can see shops with such signs as "Konditorei Hartman," "Kafee Elise," or "Hans Auto Reparatur," signaling that a private sector in services is still going strong. The survival of private small business in East Germany is a story in itself, a story that is told neither to the children nor to the adults. It is a secret story.

It all began in the postwar period of "antifascist democratic changes." As the Communist leadership inaugurated the social transformation of the GDR with land reform and nationalization of key industries, the decision was made to retain small production units in the hands of entrepreneurs known for their ability and products. Enterprises and workshops employing up to fifty workers continued to supply the kind of goods that the state simply could not produce and deliver in an efficient way. Most of the German leaders had lived quite a few years in the Soviet Union, so they knew that Stalin's radical and hasty nationalization of every sector of the economy had left a vacuum in the production of goods and services that are best suited for small establishments. So why abolish something you cannot replace?

However, this kind of rational approach does not go very well with ideological dogma. In 1971, at the Eighth Party Congress, Erich Honecker, then recently appointed first secretary, emphasized the principle of political supremacy over technocratic tendencies, which in free translation means monopoly of the party apparat over the economy. This included the elimination of certain "symptoms of capitalism." Within one year, 11,000 enterprises–including privately owned and joint state-private firms and craftsmen's cooperatives with a total of 585,000 employees–became "peoples enterprises" (*Volkseigene Betriebe*).

Very soon, however, the government was faced with a serious breakdown in services in a country where people have a daily opportunity to watch capitalism on television and compare their economic conditions with those of their counterparts in the neighboring economic giant, West Germany. A compromise solution satisfying both ideological prejudice and economic reality was eventually found. What is it?

During a recent visit to Berlin, I looked through all the bookstores and libraries in search of studies that could inform me about this particular subject. I found nothing. Finally, I was advised to go to the university's bookstore on Franzosische Strasse. There I asked the head of the department of economics for some literature dealing with small business. Again, the answer was negative. Then I insisted, "But there is such a private sector and it works." He retorted quickly, "Yes, there is a private sector and it works, but there is nothing written about it." One friend, a professor at the university, explained the internal and external reasons that make this subject taboo, *streng verboten*!–ideological prejudice and fear of being considered soft on capitalism.

The next week, it so happened that in Dresden my wife and I stumbled upon a successful entrepreneur. As we went to the Reiseburo on Prager Strasse, the clerk told us that all Interhotel rooms were booked. However, he could arrange for us to have a decent room (no bath, of course) at half price on the outskirts of Dresden, at the Hotel Freital.

The Hotel Freital has twenty-nine rooms, all clean and polished, and a cozy little restaurant. The owner, Herr M. Messer (not Micky), inherited it from his father and runs it in a sort of partnership with the state. Last summer, the hotel was reshuffled and new furniture was brought in; the state covered

60 percent of the investment and Messer contributed 40 percent. The profit is divided the same way. Messer assured us that his family lives comfortably, and his two sons (graduates of the gastronomy school) will carry on after his retirement.

Hanging on the wall of the restaurant I saw a citation *Urkunde* in which the government of the GDR, on the thirtieth anniversary of the republic, cites the merits of Messer in the management of an enterprise that serves the public interest.

The only written thing I could find about this economic policy was in the *Gesetzblatt*, the official records of the GDR in which laws and state regulations are published. Here, with German precision, are spelled out in detail the rules under which small businesses operate. In the preamble, the entrepreneurs and the lessees of restaurants, workshops, craft shops, and the like are called on to contribute to the development of services in order to help the working people in their shopping and housework. The law provides that socialist wholesale units must offer the private entrepreneurs goods under the same conditions as the socialist enterprises and to ensure their regular supply.

In the large factories, although political slogans and posters exhorting workers to participate in socialist emulation are omnipresent, the principle tying wages to performance (*Leistungsprinzip*), is a powerful incentive for higher productivity.

Agricultural policy in the 1960s profitably combined intensive modernization with the skill of the peasant; by 1973, East Germany had achieved self-sufficiency in basic foodstuffs. But then the tendency to imitate the huge Soviet *agrogorod* (agricultural towns) led to the formation of giant state farms that proved both uneconomical and unmanageable. I was told of a giant twenty-thousand-hectare state farm specializing in vegetables that was set up in the vicinity of Berlin. But at harvest time, officials discovered that harvesting carrots, herbs, and beans requires so much labor that most of the crop was lost in the field and rotted. Moreover, with the energy crisis raging, the kind of transportation and communication such large farms demand turned into a fantastic waste. Now the government, having paid a high price for its disregard of economic criteria, has decided to dismantle the big farms into smaller units. The Stalinist heritage is the most expensive item in Eastern Europe.

Having turned to small units and a policy of strong incentives for better and smarter work in agriculture, East Germany has achieved, according to the last five-year plan, among the highest productivity in Europe both in grains and in livestock. With almost five tons of grains per hectare, the 1985 crop attained 31.1 million tons of grains, which is exceptional for a population of less than 20 million people. As for animals and dairy products, output per capita is close to that of France. Small wonder that Mikhail Gorbachev has his eyes on the East German economy.

In the aftermath of World War II, Communist leaders in Eastern Europe felt that the safest thing to do was to adopt the Soviet model. Today the situation has been reversed. It is the Soviets who are bound to learn from the successful experience of Hungary, Bulgaria, and the GDR if they want to overcome the difficulties besetting their great nation.

WHAT IS ECONOMIC REFORM IN A SOCIALIST COUNTRY?

The Stalinist economic model is chiefly a politico-ideological construct in which social (the ruling class or group) and political (monopoly of power) considerations prevail over economic ones, forcing the economy to function according to vested social and political interests. Therefore, the proposal for economic reform is designed first and foremost to reinstate the primacy of economic criteria in the organization and function of the socialist economy. This very fact requires such alterations in the social and political fabric of the nation as to allow the economy to function naturally on the basis of its own motive forces and logic—that is, to function as a self-regulating mechanism.

In order to initiate properly an economic reform, the question of the economic laws and categories that operate in the transition period must first be clarified. Even in the early 1920s, Preobrazhenskii and other Soviet economists emphasized the importance of the law of value in the transition period. In fact, the whole Leninist conception of the NEP was based on the assumption that the law of value must be adequately taken into account if industrial and agricultural production is to increase and develop normally. Even Stalin, shortly before his death, admitted that the law of value operates in the Soviet economy, that in the sphere of circulation and distribution of commodities, particularly consumer goods, the law of value retains—within certain limits, to be sure—a regulating role. Moreover, it extends its influence also over the production of commodities, concluded Stalin.[28] Indeed, as long as commodities and commodity production continue to exist, the law of value will operate in the economy; this means that it is a characteristic feature of the transition period. Commodity production cannot be suppressed artificially; it will gradually disappear to the extent that the economy becomes capable of guaranteeing each member of society his basic needs so that distribution no longer has to be based on exchange.

It is characteristic of Stalin that even after admitting theoretically the role played by the law of value in socialist economy, he continued his coercive policies of acquisition, compelling the kolkhoz to surrender annually a major part of the produce to the state at very low prices. As for the consumer goods industries, they continued to produce shabby shoes and clothing without paying any attention to the demands of the consumers.

Stalin presented his model as the only possible one for a socialist economy; it is only natural, therefore, that the model should have been adopted by all East European nations after World War II. In fact, the conviction was rooted in the theoretical and ideological outlook of the revolutionary movement everywhere (including, as we will see later, that of U.S. Marxists) that the socialist economy is centrally planned not only generally but in all its elements. Accordingly, the market mechanism (implicitly, the operation of the law of value) was viewed as a foreign body in the socialist system that must be tolerated for a short period but that should at all costs be eliminated as soon as feasible.[29]

Ever since, the theoretical controversy over economic policies in socialist countries has revolved around the basic issue of plan or market. Over time, however, the discussion had to be broadened to include such issues as centralization or decentralization of economic decisions and administrative versus economic means of running the economy. Actually, the three issues are not separate and cannot be considered in isolation; they are interdependent and interact with each other, thus revealing the interlinkages between economic and political factors in the workings of a socialist economic system.

The accompanying table represents a rough outline of the situation and will be used to illustrate the discussion.

Economic Option	*Decision Making*	*Governance By*
Plan	Centralized	Administrative means
Market	Decentralized	Economic means

Simply, the table shows that the state plan (in Russian, *Gosplan*) requires a centralized system of decision making and, as a rule, administrative means to enforce decisions. The market option, on the other hand, presupposes decentralization of decision making—with a focus on the level where information about the market is available—and must use economic rather than administrative means to deal adequately with market forces.

There is a third option: a mixed economic model, with the plan governing the macroeconomic level and market relations regulating the other levels of the economy. Each respective level would then require a corresponding system of decision making and the adequate means for running it.

Surely, central planning in a socialist economy is a must. As Brus put it:

> The progressive socialization of production which finds expression both in the concentration of manufacturing in larger and larger factories and in the development of the social distribution of labor, and hence in the establishment of a complex network of economic interrelations—local, national, and international—demands an ever increasing degree of unity of direction, the co-ordination of different centers and the application of extensive criteria of rationality.[30]

However, even in 1921 Lenin realized that the use of market forms (dictated by the law of value) in the mechanism of the state plan does not necessarily mean the abandonment of central planning. Succinctly stated, his formula was: "the new economic policy *does not change* the unified state economic plan and *does not go beyond* its framework, but it alters the *means* by which it is realized."[31]

We should also consider that under Soviet conditions, the apparent contradiction between plan and market reflects in ideological terms a deeper contradiction that is fundamental and real during the transition period—the contradiction between the relations of production and the productive forces. The more backward a country, the deeper this contradiction, and of course the longer it will take to overcome it. Indeed, socialist relations of production may assert themselves only when productive forces have achieved a certain level of development. Stalin's fundamental economic law of socialism (ensuring the maximum satisfaction of the ever-growing material and cultural needs of the society through the uninterrupted growth and improvement of socialist production on the basis of the highest technology) contributed to the confusion when proceeding from the assumption that a socialist economy (or a new mode of production) was already in place.[32]

Therefore, my starting point is that we are actually dealing with an economy in a period of transition from capitalism to communism and, hence, that the new mode of production, different from the capitalist one, will take shape only at the end of that period. In the meantime, varied and even contradictory economic forms will emerge, sometimes clashing with each other, as one would expect in a society still made up of classes with different interests—an aspect clearly illustrated by the current wrangling in Eastern Europe about agricultural prices affecting the purchasing power of the working class.

As long as commodities and commodity production exist, the law of value will operate in the economy, which means that the law of value is a characteristic feature of the entire transition period. The law of value is inextricably linked with the commodity-money relationship, for the action of the law of value is such that the relations of value are defined by the relationship of prices; consequently, there is a constant tendency, an objective pressure, to bring price relations to relations of value, and there is no other way for these operations to express themselves except through money.

An important theoretical point here is that commodity production and the law of value that goes with it normally cover the industrial sector of consumer goods and agriculture. As for the industries of capital goods, once they are nationalized, their products lose the character of commodities and acquire use value. Although these products are formally sold (or exchanged) by one state enterprise to another, this is merely a bookkeeping operation and a general verification of the execution of the plan and of the economy as a whole—a procedure that is expressed also in the particular monetary form of bank papers involving no cash.

Although the capital goods industries can be effectively run by the state plan, the production of the consumer goods industries and of agriculture must be regulated by the law of value; the plan can do no more than try to set some limits to its action. This is why some Marxist economists have criticized the Stalinist model and have argued instead in favor of a model of a planned economy with a regulated (or built-in) market mechanism as the best solution to accommodate the different economic sectors (or levels) during the transition period.[33]

Politics First

Having dealt with the theory of economic categories, let me emphasize that in practice, economic categories have been thoroughly underestimated or suffocated altogether by heavy-handed planning and administrative coercion. It all began, of course, with war communism.

Although economically war communism brought the nation to the brink of disaster, the Bolsheviks took pride in this period when the defeat everybody expected was turned into victory. From that point on, the heroic period of war communism retained its symbolic presence in all subsequent economic policy debates, establishing a sort of tradition in the relationship between political and economic criteria in decision making, with politics enjoying indisputable priority over economics. This in itself set the stage for the way economic categories would be treated by the Soviet leadership in years to come.

Usually official documents and textbooks on economics emphasize that party economic policy is always scientifically substantiated and that, accordingly, the five-year plans are always based on a careful study of the economic laws and categories operating in the USSR. In fact, it is political considerations that prevail in economic decisions, from investment policy to the orientation of foreign trade.

Certainly, it was not the study of the operation of the law of value in agriculture that made Stalin dictate his "extraordinary measures"—the harsh grain procurement and collection campaigns and eventually the forced collectivization offensive. The kolkhoz itself, as conceived by Stalin, was a most drastic denial of economic laws in agriculture. Although theoretically it was declared a cooperative form of ownership distinct from the state farm, in practice the kolkhoz was treated as a state enterprise, compelled to produce for the state what the state ordered it to produce on conditions set by the state. Official pronouncements that there should be mercantile relations between the kolkhoz and the state are in fact contradicted by the actual appropriation of farm products through state acquisitions and price policies. In most cases, prices are so fixed that they do not even cover the cost of production. The motivation, of course, is again political: Because of the low wages of the workers, the state must provide them with basic food items (bread, meat, milk, butter, and the like) at low prices and, therefore, the prices paid to the kolkhoz must be even lower. Small wonder that even in years when the climate is extremely favorable, resulting in bumper crops, 15 to 20 percent of the grains remain in the field unharvested in spite of the formidable party mobilization and the calls for socialist emulation.

The entire agricultural policy, from the forced collectivization campaign to present-day measures, has been formulated in clear defiance of Marx's warning that the law of value has an objective character that "asserts itself by force, like a natural regulating law, in the same manner as, for example, the law of gravitation asserts itself when the house falls upon you."[34] The best illustration of this is the size of the black market in the socialist countries. The black market in food and consumer goods is in fact the economic form whereby the law of value tries to reassert its action against policies that try to suppress it.

It is worth mentioning here that in China also, after the disastrous experience of the Cultural Revolution, the need has been strongly underlined to study and observe economic laws. A leading Chinese scholar has this to say: "They have gone so far as to imagine that it is possible to put politics in command while neglecting objective economic laws and that acknowledgment of economic laws means negating politics in command. This view is entirely wrong. We must treat the two things separately."[35]

The very logic of command-type planning rejects economic categories whose actions do not conform to the plan. Value, money, commodity, market, and so on are thus perceived by the planners as economic categories that are in adversary relationships with the almighty *Gosplan*, hindering or obstructing its beneficial effects. Small wonder that for twenty years—from 1929, when the first five-year plan was launched, to 1951, Stalin's meeting with the economists—economic categories constituted a subversive subject of conversation. Not until Stalin's death was there public discussion of that issue.

The Social Facet

To go deeper into the issue of economic reform, we have to deal with the crux of the matter—the class or social group wielding power.

In discussing economic categories in the USSR, Charles Bettelheim noted that the contradiction between plan and market would persist throughout the transition period, and he emphasized that the decisive factor is not economic but political. He rejected the idea that the existence of the market is an impelling force leading toward the restoration of capitalism—an argument that has been invoked time and again by Stalinist-minded theoreticians against the Yugoslav reform in the 1950s, against the Prague Spring in 1968, and against the "capitalist roaders" by the Gang of Four during the Cultural Revolution in China. "In reality," pointed out Bettelheim, "this is not so. Everything depends on the manner in which it [the plan or market] is dealt with, and this manner depends on class relations, including those existing at the ideological level."[36]

In order to identify better the political and social sides of the economic reform, we will have to reconstruct the historical process whereby economic policies in the postrevolutionary Soviet Union intertwined and interacted with social and political developments; eventually all these factors were lumped together in a unique and peculiar system whose structure and patterns of behavior crystallized so strongly over time that the parts became inseparable from the whole.

As we noted earlier, as early as 1918 the politics of war communism—with its complete "socialization" of production and labor, requisitioning in the countryside, and strict rationing for the urban population—resulted in the extensive bureaucratic concentration of economic life, requiring a vast and numerous bureaucracy to run all these operations. By 1920, the number of bureaucrats in relation to production workers was twice that under the czarist regime. Indeed, once in power, the Bolshevik party could not operate in a vacuum: Since the proletariat was the missing link of the grand revolutionary design, the party had to rely ever more on the state and its apparat to consolidate its power and to enforce its policies and decisions. At that time, Lenin, though he warned against the "bureaucratic state," did not and could not anticipate that this kind of state system would influence deeply the very character of the economic base it was supposed to uplift; even less did he foresee that the apparat, once invested with such tremendous powers over the economy and once accustomed to deciding almost every economic problem without having to consult a social base, would resist any challenge to its monopoly of economic power, any attempt to decentralize or democratize the economic system.

The formation of such an economic system was strengthened, or perhaps facilitated, by the fact that the state form of ownership does not allow workers to exercise their property rights directly—that is, to achieve what Marx called "the domination of producers over their conditions of existence;"[37] instead, these rights were necessarily taken over by a professional, skilled group of people: the economic state bureaucrats. Under Stalin, the bureaucracy of the state gradually merged with that of the party, thus becoming the key factor in shaping the whole system.

It was the vanguard of the working class—that is, the Bolshevik party—that got hold of power, and not the working class as a whole. We should recall that in the French Revolution also it was a dedicated and ideologically motivated group, a minority party to be sure—the Montagnard Jacobins—that came to power as a result of their success in mobilizing and channeling the discontent and fighting fervor of the *sans culottes*.

Indeed, never in history has the emerging class as such come to power from the very inception of a revolution. Revolutions have always started with a minority group or party, more or less representative of the new class. Only afterwards, passing through various intricate stages, has the new class as a whole been able to impose its domination and become the ruling class.

The dictatorship of the proletariat, therefore, is a misnomer; it was and remains a false proposition in a backward country where not only the political party but also the class—the proletariat—represent a minority of the population. The very assumption that the proletariat, a class that is less experienced and less educated than the bourgeoisie, could from the very beginning manage the complicated state affairs and run a modern society with so complex an organization was utterly wrong theoretically and has proven equally wrong in practice. Recall that the working class, unlike the aristocracy and bourgeoisie, received the opportunity for an adequate education only after the Revolution.

Moreover, this basic theoretical error was compounded by a lack of understanding of the very logic of power. What happened in both the French and Russian revolutions was that the political vanguard, once entrenched in power and having to consolidate it through a political structure of its own, would resist any future attempt of the class it claimed to represent to play its rightful role in ruling the country.

In the meantime, a large working class has emerged in the Soviet Union. In Stalin's time, largely given to rapid industrialization, urban centers more than doubled in population; the 1939 census showed nearly 56 million people living in cities, mostly industrial workers. In other words, about 30 million people have moved from the villages to the cities, joining the industrial labor force, and I submit that it was that emerging working class that constituted the social base of the Communist party in the Stalin era. Recall that when he started the collectivization drive, Stalin could safely rely on the 25,000 industrial workers who were enrolled by the party to go into the villages as collectivizers.

The influx toward industry was largely an influx of the peasant-born leaving the dreary life of the villages and stepping into the attractive cities, getting jobs and social status full of promises. Although times were hard, with food scarce and living conditions poor, there was no comparison with what they had left behind in the rural areas. Moreover, career and educational opportunities opened up without precedent to the millions of uprooted peasants entering the new industrial plants.

The party and the state have consistently courted the new working class. Although wages have been kept depressed, basic food items have been heavily subsidized by the state to stubbornly maintain their low prices over years and decades. Millions of new apartments have been built for industrial workers, with rents set very low; public utilities (electricity, gas, heating, water) and transportation remain very cheap. If we add to all these what is called the "social salary"—free education, health care, bonuses, and tickets for health resorts and vacations on the Black Sea—we begin to understand the stability of the regime in the USSR.

However, in recent decades it has become increasingly clear that the working class in Eastern Europe is demanding much more than the regime offers. In fact, the uprising in Hungary (1956), the Prague Spring (1968), and the strong social movement in Poland (1980) tell us in a contradictory and at times awkward way that the working class is no longer willing to accept the situation in which a small and privileged group exercises power on its behalf. The workers feel they are now sufficiently educated and mature to take power as a ruling class. It is this fundamental social demand that the economic reform must meet if it is to succeed in all its articulations. Essentially, we are talking here about installing socialist democracy in both its economic and political facets.

Workers' democracy at the factory level has more than political relevance: It constitutes a most essential element of socialist relations of production. Without it, socialist ownership is deprived of avenues through which the will and the interests of the proletariat can be expressed in the running of the productive apparatus, and instead degenerates into an empty formal juridical definition that lacks historical and practical importance.

The domination of producers over the means of production constitutes the essence of socialist relations of production. Progress on the path to socialism requires, therefore, such a transformation of the forms of this domination that it becomes increasingly complete. It is in this sense that the class struggle in a postrevolutionary society becomes significant; its major task is to revolutionize the various economic, ideological, and political mechanisms with the goal of eliminating and replacing the capitalist social relations that continue to reproduce themselves. The end of this process is the direct participation of producers in the management of enterprises.

One final point: Anti-reformers in the East argue that in both Hungary and China the unleashed market forces have generated not only a sharp rise in agricultural production but also serious problems–social and ideological. Those in favor of change answer that serious problems of that nature also exist under rigid state planning (black marketeering, corruption, alcoholism, and embezzlement, to name but a few) and that, in the last analysis, the choice is between problems arising from shortages and those arising from surplus. Those in favor of change conclude that socialism naturally should go for the surplus.

NOTES

1. V. Trapeznikov, "Direction of Technological-Scientific Progress," *Pravda*, 1982, no. 127.
2. *Planovoie Hozeaistvo*, Moscow, no. 9 (1979): 30.
3. Ibid., 41.
4. "Ekonomicheskie Problemi naucheno-technicheskoi politiki," *Planovoie Hozeaistvo*, no. 9 (1979): 109.
5. *Problemi Narodnoie–hozeaistvenogo optimiuma* pot redaktzii K.K. Valtuch, Novosibirsk, 206.
6. *Ekonomika i Matematicheskie Metodi*, no. 1 (1980): 88.
7. *Statistical Abstracts of the United States*, 1975, 760.
8. *Narodnoe Hoziastvo Stran Cilenov* (Moscow, 1978), 97.
9. *Pravda*, 16 June 1983, 1.
10. Tatyana Zaslavkaya, Doklad o neobkhodimosti bolee uglubennogo izucheniya v SSSR sotzial-nogo mekhanisma razvityia ekonomiki, AS 5042, 22 August 1983.
11. See *EKO*, no. 5 (1980): 44; and *Voprosi Ekonomiki*, no. 2 (1978): 39; No. 7 (1979): 36; no. 10 (1979): 47; and no. 7 (1984): 53.
12. Mikhail Gorbachev, Political Report of the CPSU Central Committee to the 27th Congress of the CPSU, *New Times*, Moscow, 10 March 1986.

13. See Loren R. Graham, *Science and Philosophy in the Soviet Union* (New York: Knopf, 1971), 336-7.

14. Extrapolated from the data calculated by the World Bank for the years 1955 and 1980; see *World Development Report* (Washington, D.C., 1982), 22.

15. See *Narodnoie Hozeaistvo SSSR, 1922-1982* (Moscow, 1983).

16. Peter Drucker, "Our Entrepreneurial Economy," *Harvard Business Review*, 1984.

17. *The Economist*, London, 24 December 1983, 59-61.

18. *Economic Impact*, Washington D.C., no. 47 (1984): 61.

19. *Narodnoie Hozeaistvo SSSR* (1982): 89, 372.

20. See *Soviet Economy Today* prepared by Novosti, Moscow, (Connecticut: Greenwood Press, 1981), 161-163.

21. Production figures on grains and livestock have been subject to successive changes over the years in Soviet statistics; I have chosen the figures as they were revised after Khrushchev's revelations, and they seemed to me consistent with the evolution of Soviet agriculture on the basis of statistics published by *Sel'skoie Khozyaistvo SSSR* stat, sbornik (Moscow, 1960: 79, and 1971: 33d); and *Narodnoekhozyiaistvo SSR* v. 1958 (Moscow, 1959: 350).

22. Ibid.

23. Ibid.

24. Ibid.

25. *Pravda*, 22 October 1980.

26. *Critique*, Glasgow, no. 16.

27. *Statistischeskii ejegodnik SEV* (1981): 216.

28. I. V. Stalin, *Economic Problems in the USSR* (Moscow, 1951).

29. Wlodzimierz Brus, *The Market in a Socialist Economy* (London: Routledge & Kegan Paul, 1972), 27.

30. Ibid. 8, see also M. Ya Kaziev, ed. *Gosudarstvennoie sotsialnoe strakovanie* (Moscow: Profizdat, 1965).

31. V. I. Lenin, *Opere* (Bucharest: Editura Politica, 1962), 123.

32. On the market issue the international discussion was particularly vivid. Interestingly, U.S. Marxists who have seen the worst effects of the law of the market, particularly at the time of the depression, sharply criticized Yugoslav theory and practice almost in the same vein as the Soviet critiques of that theory. In *Monthly Review* (March 1964), an article bearing the striking title "Transition from Socialism to Capital-

ism?" vigorously attacked the use of market mechanisms and ended with the dramatic appeal: "Beware of the market–it is the secret weapon of capitalism." Years later, Paul Sweezy warned that Eastern Europe is leaning toward economic reform: "The contention is that whoever acts to strengthen the market is, regardless of intention, promoting capitalism and not socialism." He maintained that the market course was adopted "not because the bureaucracies had any love for the capitalist methods but because they could see no other way to preserve their power and privileges" ("Czechoslovakia, Capitalism and Socialism," *Monthly Review*, October 1968). This showed, among other things, that politico-ideological considerations may strongly affect economic judgment; in fact, the article appeared at a time when Soviet tanks were killing the Prague Spring economic reform, and in the Kremlin even the timid Kosygin reforms were rescinded, reinstating the power of the apparat over the economy.

33. Challenged by Charles Bettelheim, Sweezy amended his earlier position and stated that "The view I do hold is that market relationships (which of course imply money and prices) are inevitable under socialism for a long time, but that they constitute a standing danger to the system and unless strictly hedged in and controlled will lead to degeneration and repression" (*Monthly Review*, March 1969).

Commenting on these reactions, W. Brus wrote that they "are based on the erroneous idea that plan and market are mutually exclusive economic institutions. The plan is identified with a system in which directives are enforced by orders, while the market is thought of as a spontaneously self-regulating mechanism which by definition precluded the social handling of economic processes. These ideas I believe to be wrong. Socialist planning is the conscious allocation of resources in order to achieve the maximum satisfaction of social needs. It is to this end that the institutions of a planned economy must be subordinated–nor is the command system of the centralized economy the only form which such institutions may take. In some circumstances a regulated market mechanism is (or may at least appear to be) the form better suited to a planned economy than a command mechanism." Brus went on, arguing that when the growth of a socialist economy makes its structures more complex, the use of the market is not to ensure the success of the plan (*The Economics and Politics of Socialism*, London: Routledge & Kegan Paul, 1973, 35). At the same time, Brus also warned that "one of the most important things to remember when employing the market mechanism in a planned socialist economy is that the commercial provision of consumer goods and services must be limited. A failure to do so would be to fall victim to commodity fetishism" (p. 64).

Bettelheim brought into the discussion the political and social side of the issue: "What characterizes socialism as opposed to capitalism is not the existence or nonexistence of market relationships, money and prices, but the existence of the domination of the proletariat, of the dictatorship of the proletariat. It is through the exercise of this dictatorship in all areas–economic, political, ideological–that market relations can be progressively eliminated by means of concrete measures adapted to concrete situations and conjunctures. This elimination cannot be decreed or proclaimed. It requires political strategy and tactics" (*Monthly Review*, March 1969).

On this issue see also Ernest Mandel, "Marxist Economic Theory," *Monthly Review*, 1969. The theoretical conclusion of his discussion is that the Marxist method cannot be reduced either to a strictly economic interpretation or to an exclusively political vision primarily based on class conflict at a given time. Actually, Marx's specific contribution to social theory is his holistic approach linking economic conditions with political and ideological factors in a systemic paradigm that allows each to have a preponderant influence upon the course of events, depending upon historical circumstances. However, there is an interaction among these factors compelling them to adjust to each other's movement and ultimately to that of the economic factor, which remains decisive in the long run.

34. K. Marx, *Opere*, vol. 23 (Bucharest: Editura Politica, 1965), 108.

35. Hu Chiao-mu, president of the Chinese Academy of Social Sciences, "Observe Economic Laws, Speed-Up the Four Modernizations," *Peking Review*, no. 45 (1978).

36. Charles Bettelheim, "On the Transition Between Capitalism and Socialism," *Monthly Review* (March 1969).

37. A distinction should be made between nationalization of the means of production, which means that the state is becoming their owner and manager, and socialization, which presupposes the domination of producers over the means of production–that is, the direct participation of the working class in the management of enterprises. Ac-

cording to Oscar Lange, "Socialist ownership of the means of production involves both the use of the means of production in the interests of society as a whole and effective democratic participation by producers and other workers in the management of the means of production" (*Economic and Social Papers*, Warsaw, 1961). The identification of nationalization with socialization in the political economy of Eastern Europe has led to theoretical confusion; it constitutes one of the basic misconceptions that have hindered the formulation of a consistent and coherent theory of the socialist economic system.

3

THE FUTURE

WHERE IS SOCIALISM HEADING?

The crisis of socialist theoretical thought brought about by stubbornly clinging to Stalin's political structures and ideological dogmas (which have never been critically reexamined) is nowhere as apparent as in the approach to the problems of future Communist society. The future of human society, the future of the world in general, is discussed very seldom in the East; there are few books about such an important subject and no model for the year 2000—a striking paradox for societies supposed to march into the future and to embody the hopes of men for a better society. Half a century of strict thought control is striking back with a vengeance. And yet, the question remains: Where are we going? Where is socialism heading?

Stalin's pretense that all his plans were scientifically elaborated, based on objective laws of social development, has been inherited by all Communist leaders in the past. That pretense was categorically destroyed by Khrushchev's 1961 Program of the Soviet Communist Party, unanimously adopted by the Twenty-second Congress. The program proclaimed: "In the current decade (1961-70) the Soviet Union, in creating the material and technical basis of communism, will surpass the strongest and richest capitalist country, the U.S.A., in production per head of population." It went further: "The material and technical basis of communism will be built up by the end of the second decade (1971-80), ensuring an abundance of material and cultural values for the whole population. Soviet society will come close to a stage where it can introduce the principle of distribution according to need and there will be a gradual transition to one form of ownership—public ownership. Thus, a communist society will in the main be built in the USSR."[1]

We are now in 1987 and the Soviets are far from those predictions. Theoretically, an essential element was missing in this fantastic program, and that is the *new type of productive forces* that will usher in the formation of the new mode of production characteristic of Communist society. Let us recall Marx's retrospective historical scheme: The primitive society uses stone tools, the slave system uses metallic tools, the feudal system uses the mill set in motion by people, trade, and manufacture, while capitalism started with machines, particularly the steam engine.[2] What about communism? Here, the condition of underdevelopment provided by the Russian environment left its mark on Lenin's thinking as he said: "The century of steam was the bourgeois century, the century of electric power is the socialist century."[3]

Certainly, capitalist economies have not been short of electric power; they started using it long before the October Revolution and continue to do so without any limitation. Therefore, electricity could hardly be viewed as the new productive force for communism. On 9 February 1946, speaking at an election meeting, Stalin pointed out that the USSR should reach such a level of productive forces that the annual output would be about 50 million tons of pig iron, 60 million tons of steel, 500 million tons of coal, and about 60 million tons of oil; from that point on this became the level at which the material basis of communism would be built.[4] In 1961, Khrushchev defined the matter as "the bone and muscular system of machines for the complex mechanization and automation," and he emphasized, "The Leninist idea of total electrification constitutes the pivot of the whole program of construction of a communist economy."[5]

But again, all this has been incorporated in the West without restrictions imposed by the system. Therefore, it cannot constitute the bone and muscle system of a future mode of production and society at a time when the most advanced capitalist countries, the United States and Japan, are stepping into the age of computerization and information, microelectronics and robots. It is this basic handicap and the unanswerable question it raises that explain why there is so little debate in the East about the future of society and of the world. This chapter will explore the significance and implications of that abnormal situation.

Before going on I would like to point out what I consider to be the crux of the problem. Characteristic of Lenin's and Khrushchev's anticipations is the assumption that the main goal of socialism is industrialization and therefore Communist society's mode of production should be based on the most advanced machine tools of the industrial system. In fact, industrialization historically belongs to the capitalist epoch. The construction of a modern industry should constitute at best the premise of a socialist society rather than its goal. To advance toward communism a mode of production must be built surpassing the limits of the industrial system. Today, communism should be viewed as a postindustrial society.

It is not fortuitous that the most serious studies and discussions on the postindustrial society originate in Japan, the most advanced country in high technology. As early as 1972 a special institute was set up in Tokyo with the view of elaborating a program for "the creation of an information society as a postindustrial society"—proclaimed as the national objective of Japan for the year 2000. The fundamental assumption is that the combination of computers with telecommunications will generate a new social technology of *information*, thus replacing the production of material goods characteristic of industrial society. This will require a qualitative change in human values, the direction of thinking, and the economic and political structure of society, and will also include the transformation of representative parliamentary democracy into participatory democracy, with citizens participating directly in decision making.* Although the program ignores the con-

*Yoneji Masuda, *The Information Society as Post-Industrial Society*, Institute for Information Society (I.I.S.), Tokyo, 1980.

tradictions at both national and international levels and the dynamics of power that such a change would have to overcome, it is interesting that Japanese futurologists have concluded that the new society would have to surpass the capitalist system based on competition between private enterprises, the profit motive, commodity production, and the law of supply and demand; capitalism could not solve the problem of unemployment engendered by complex automation. Indeed, the new revolutionary technologies illustrate once more the dialectical law that social phenomena will perish as a result of their own development. It is in this perspective that the debate on Communist society should be undertaken today, with the proviso that the new revolution in technology first must be mastered.

TOO LITTLE FOR TOO MUCH

The new party program adopted by the CPSU's 1986 Congress has dropped the bombastic tone of the previous program, using a more realistic approach in defining both the USSR's current state (just entering the stage of developed socialism) and the tasks that lay ahead (the planned and all-round perfection of socialism). Referring to the "groundless fantasies" (Gorbachev) of the old program, it emphasizes that "attempts to move ahead too fast and to introduce communist principles without taking into consideration the level of material and spiritual maturity of society are, as experience has shown, doomed to failure and may cause both economic and political losses."[6]

Lenin said once that what distinguishes the Communist party from other political parties is its courage to admit mistakes in order to correct them. This seems to have been a hard rule to follow; a political myth has been created over the years claiming that the party has always been right. The new program is paying due respect to the myth: "The time that has elapsed since the Third Program was adopted [1961] has confirmed the correctness of its main theoretical and political propositions." We may ask, then, why these propositions have been criticized and changed. Given that tradition has been piously respected, a telling difference appears in the new program from the unblemished and uniformly wise party policy depicted by previous documents. Virtually all predecessors except Lenin are criticized: "The party did a great deal to eliminate the consequences of the personality cult, deviations from the Leninist norms of Party and state guidance," referring clearly to Stalin's abuses of power, "and to rectify errors of subjectivist, voluntaristic nature," the sins usually attributed to Khrushchev.[7] Of course, no names are mentioned.

But the main target of the criticism is directed against the Brezhnev era, the seventies and early eighties. This era is blamed for "the failure to assess appropriately and in good time, changes in the economic situation and the need for profound transformations in all spheres of life."[8] Those were the years when, as I mentioned earlier, the West's ability to assimilate the scientific-technological revolution resulted in a tremendous expansion of productive forces, leaving behind the economies of the USSR and other socialist countries. Apparently the new generation coming to power in Moscow is aware of that widening East-West gap and is determined to do something about it.

From the very beginning the new leader, Mikhail Gorbachev, spoke of the need for "fundamental changes in the economy and in the whole system of social relations." At the party Congress he mentioned an in-depth readjustment of the economic mechanism and pointed out, "the situation today is such that we cannot limit ourselves to partial improvements. A radical reform is needed."[9]

However, his rhetoric appears more radical than his practical policies. For the time being, the emphasis remains on

Gorbachev's two-track policy—reassuring the party bureaucracy of its centralized power and at the same time giving managers of local enterprises a greater say in production and stimulation of workers' performance—as a local saying goes, "trying to reconcile the goat with the cabbage."

This approach has been tested in 1984 with the "industrial experiment" in five key ministries, which will be extended in 1987 to all factories. The number of directives issued by the state planning agency Gosplan has been sharply reduced; enterprises have been given the right to produce and sell new commodities from waste products and raw materials allotted to them once they fulfill their planned quotas. Profits from these new ventures are to be retained by the enterprise and used either for investment, social services, or bonuses to encourage innovation. At the same time, a new law considerably expands the powers of workers' councils in such matters as economic planning, pay, bonuses, and the monitoring of management activities. Assessing the results of the experiment, Soviet economists note some progress but, as Abel Aganbegyan, head of the Novosibirsk Institute, emphasized in *Izvestia* (April 1985), "there has been no breakthrough in productivity."

Indeed, there is an obvious disproportion between the magnitude of the problem attributed to Brezhnev's failure to grasp the significance of the scientific-technological revolution and the timid measures suggested to deal with that problem. Although the key word of the whole economic program is *acceleration*, to regain lost ground, the Soviet leader seems to move very cautiously when it comes to the pillars of the old system. He is probably right to do so, for a radical reform would have to break not only the stubborn resistance of party bureaucrats, but also the reluctance of many managers to make decisions that carry risks, and above all the deeply entrenched mentality of the mass of workers that they should enjoy job security, equal pay, and bonuses regardless of their work performance.

But Gorbachev made two important theoretical points opening up the prospect of a radical reform. He categorically rejected the main ideological shibboleth of conservative hardliners that "any change in the economic mechanism should be regarded as being practically a retreat from the principles of socialism."[10] He also pointed out the fallacy of the "ideas that under conditions of socialism the conformity of production relations to the nature of the productive forces is ensured automatically, as it were."[11] He added that "outdated economic management methods must be noticed in good time and replaced by new ones."[12]

Many leading Soviet economists are speaking publicly in favor of reform. Even the director of the Gosplan Institute of Economics Vadim Kirichenko, in *New Times*, 20 January, 1986, criticized the assumption that all branches of the economy are similar as objects of planning and argued the case of a mixed system without naming Hungary. Whereas he concedes that in the basic branches directive planning will not change, he writes, "in consumer goods the production output of most products cannot be determined by centralized planning. In this sphere, the range of products should be prompted by consumer preferences, first and foremost."

As for agriculture, a March 1986 decision of the Central Committee and government provides strong material incentives for better performance: state output of the previous five-year plan will be doubled; pay for better individual performance in cooperatives and state farms will be considerably higher; and animal products of private farms and household plots can be sold on the free market. The role of family households will be greatly enhanced and, following the example of Hungary, collective farms will entrust most of their animals to subsidiary small holdings for raising or fattening.[13]

Probably the most difficult reform for the Soviet system is renouncing the administrative method that is the very essence of Stalin's command economy and relying instead on economic means in managing the production process. This affects not only the party bureaucracy's power and privileges, but also the managers who were relieved of responsibility and risk and the mass of workers enjoying equal pay regardless of their individual performance. There is now official admission that in the consumer goods industries and agriculture it is the law of value that regulates production and distribution and, therefore, directive must be replaced with incentive as a modus operandi. The administrative method has resulted in food shortages, poor services, and shabby consumer goods that, as Gorbachev put it, are produced mostly for the warehouses. Since the light industry production now must meet consumer demand, a feverish activity is under way to brighten the drab look of Soviet fashion. Moda (meaning fashion, in Russian) is Moscow's hottest new store offering quality clothing with attractive designs and fabrics; the line of customers stretching for blocks is evidence of its success. To get a quick haute couture fix, famous manufacturers from abroad such as Pierre Cardin and Yves Saint Laurent have been invited to design clothes and sell them in Soviet shops. A new system of incentives will reward plants and workers who produce popular garments.

The vast gray area of Soviet law and economy covering services and small business that has been generating the black market and various forms of private earnings considered illegal has finally been elucidated by the new law on individual labor adopted in November 1986 by the Supreme Soviet. Twenty-nine types of private businesses, ranging from cafes to shoemakers and repair shops, will be allowed to operate with state aid, including bank loans, and under state control offering services and goods that the government cannot provide or provides very poorly. Each private business will be run by a family, hiring of workers being forbidden; taxes will be paid according to estimates of profits made by authorities. In addition, experiments are encouraged for cooperatives of five to fifty members that will run either a restaurant or a workshop or can collect and process secondary raw materials and production waste such as leather, wood, or woolens. Such a cafe in Tallin, Estonia, was praised in the media for its success in employing half the staff and attracting twice the clientele that it did when it was state-run. Although the Soviet government has resolved to make the consumer happier, there is real concern to avoid the negative effect experienced in Hungary, where the reform produced a massive exodus of highly skilled workers to the private sector and a lower performance in the state economy.

The egalitarian tradition in wage policy is still going strong. A vast social inquiry in early 1986 concluded that only a third of industrial workers make a real effort to do a good job, with most of them getting the same wage as the lazy workers. Another study reveals that many young engineers prefer to get hired as workers to earn more money. Speaking about the directive to set wages according to the quantity and quality of work, Gorbachev criticized the Ministry of Apparatus Construction for distorting the directive by adding a few rubles for everybody, regardless of individual performance. He praised, however, the action taken in Leningrad's research institutes, where inefficient employees were fired; although the number of engineers was reduced by a third, many more finished projects have been recorded, their quality has been improved, and as a result the earnings of their makers has doubled and tripled.

Finally, dramatic changes were announced in October 1986 for Soviet foreign trade. The ministry's monopoly control over exports and imports was terminated. Twenty-one ministries and sixty-seven major enterprises are authorized to negotiate and sign contracts with foreign companies. To encourage joint ventures, the USSR is allowing foreign corporations holding 49 percent (and Soviet companies, 51 percent) of the investment to repatriate profits, control prices, and remain free of the planning bureaucracy; the joint venture, however, will be expected to earn the foreign currency needed to compensate for the repatriation. In one year, more than twenty Western companies have signed contracts under the new regulations, including such giants as Monsanto and Occidental Petroleum.

As expected, these reforms are encountering the stubborn resistance of party and state bureaucrats at both central and middle levels. Gorbachev has been complaining in public speeches that the new measures have become mired in bureaucracy, and he has denounced those who oppose change and are unable to give up old habits and methods of command. For the first time, the Central Committee of the party has acknowledged publicly that people in power oppose change: "Although our society as a whole is firmly oriented toward change, the restructuring of the economy encounters various socio-psychological and organizational obstacles and the resistance of those who are moved by selfish interests, trying to preserve outdated rules and privileges" (*Pravda*, 1 October 1986).

Indeed, as in Hungary and China, it is increasingly clear that reform of the economy cannot be successfully carried out if political structures are not equally revamped. Here Gorbachev seems to be proceeding with prudence and tact. Even the key words are carefully selected so as not to touch sensitive ideological prejudices. Instead of reform, Gorbachev speaks of "restructuring" the economy; for the market, the current expression is "money-commodity relations"; private business in the new law was called "individual labor"; and the rapporteur emphasized that the new law in no way constitutes a departure from socialist principles.

At the same time, Gorbachev dissuades expectations that are too great and that demand quick results by declaring, "The real turning point in implementing the strategic goals set by the 27th Congress is still far away." The chairman of Gosplan, presenting the results of the 1986 economic plan, noted that there has been no breakthrough in production and productivity yet. Nor is one expected in 1987, according to the modest targets set in Gorbachev's plan. Indeed, while the growth in industrial output is moving at a 4 to 5 percent rate annually, labor productivity is rising by less than 5 percent. In agriculture, the 1986 grain crop recorded an equally modest increase: 210 million tons (260 are necessary to meet all demands). Such figures may sound satisfactory if we forget about the serious lag behind the Western economic-technological level besetting the Soviet Union. To overcome that lag, much more radical measures will be required.

A Precious Ally: The Intelligentsia

Gorbachev, faced with so much resistance in his drive to change not only the economy but also the psychology of the nation, is trying to attract the intelligentsia to his barricades. The release from exile of Andrei Sakharov is the most spectacular gesture in this direction, but the strategy started much earlier. The first signal came when Yevgeny Yevtushenko in the summer of 1985 brought to the magazine *Novy Mir* a manuscript entitled "Fuku," a virulent attack on Beria, Stalin's chief of secret police. Rejected by Glavlit, the state censorship board, "Fuku" was taken to Gorbachev, who read it and gave the green light for publication, arousing great hope among writers.

The denunciation of cultural bureaucrats has been gathering pace for some time. The poet Andrei Voznesenski fulminated in *Sovietskaya Rossiya* against the fact that "an author spends ten percent of his life writing and 90 percent on getting it published." One of the leading novelists, Vassily Bykov, mounted a real campaign in *Literaturnaya Gazeta* for the publication of *The Sad Detective* by V. Astafiev, the story of a militia officer in a small town of Belorussia who recounts his long fight against the most horrible crimes, revealing a degree of violence that has never been reported in the Soviet press.

But the most successful novel recently published after having been given the thumbs-down by Glavlit is *The Serpent Hunter* by Lazar Karelin, a sensational presentation of the underground of black marketeers, various dubious characters who deal in hard-to-get goods from caviar to Italian shoes, just about everything that is in short supply and high demand—what Russians call *defitzit*. Eventually, the government decided to abolish Glavlit, after its somber sixty-seven-year reign.

The ferment in the literary world rapidly spread to other fields. At the composers' congress, the chairman Rodion Shchedrin launched an extraordinary attack on the deputy minister of culture, Ivanov, describing him as a poor administrator who knew nothing of music. At the conference of filmmakers, the younger members pulled off a tactical coup by electing one of their own, film director Elem Klimov, as first secretary. Klimov's first decision was to set up a commission to review all the films that had been left to rot on the shelf, unscreened, a fate which some of his own work (the film *Agonia*, called *Rasputin* in the West) had shared. Leading actors and directors of Moscow theaters joined the discussion. Oleg Efremov, director of the prestigious MHAT Theater, in a *Pravda* article lashed at the *kulturnik aparatchiki* who are interfering incompetently in the texts and presentation of the plays. Mark Zakharov, director of the Komsomol Theater, pointed out that two main ingredients are essential for the success of the reform: a change of attitude renouncing the suspicion and lack of trust toward the Soviet intelligentsia and an acceptance of the fact that in every artistic endeavor there is an element of risk.

The climax of the reform movement was the June congress of the Writer's Union. It began with the election as secretary general of Vladimir Karpov, who had been imprisoned by Stalin for criticizing the cult of personality. Then some of the most daring poets and writers (Akhmadulina, Bulat Okudjava, and Yuri Chernichenko), whose election as delegates to the congress had been obstructed by local party organs, were elected by acclamation to the presidium of the congress. After stormy debates in which censorship, uncalled-for interference of bureaucrats, and cultural repression came under sharp criticism, nine of the Soviet Union's best writers held an unusual press conference to make the dramatic announcement that Boris Pasternak, who had been expelled from the union thirty years ago, would be honored by the making of his house into a museum and the publication of his works, including *Dr. Zhivago*.

What distinguishes the present thaw from Khrushchev's is the movement from below so apparent in the resurgent membership of the creative unions. This is what democracy is all about. Yevtushenko made this point clearly: "The reform must not come as a gift from above; we are the ones to bring it about. Through the Union we will henceforth try to use our own power to defend the books of our comrades and brothers against the bureaucracy." He and Vosnesenski have gone through a hard experience and have learned that reform from above is limited in substance and duration and therefore may well be followed by a conservative backlash, as happened under Brezhnev. The tendency of creative unions–particularly those of writers, filmmakers, playwrights, and composers–to become independent constitutes a much more significant political phenomenon than the progressive measures taken by the leadership, though in the Soviet system the eruption in the unions so widely reported in the press could hardly take place without the encouraging signals from Mikhail Gorbachev.

ECONOMIC REFORM IN THE EAST: A STRATEGIC ISSUE

Having dealt with the domestic stimuli and restrictions of economic reform, I anticipate that the degree and speed of change in the Soviet system will be determined chiefly by strategic considerations. The strategic position of CMEA in the world economy is defined by three percentages: roughly 36 percent of all world industrial production, but only 11 percent of world trade and merely 9 percent of world financial transactions. This reveals a low competitiveness in industrial products and a limited capability to influence processes on the world market. The Soviet Union is the largest world oil producer and yet, in the spring of 1986 when the price of oil dropped substantially on world markets, the Soviets could do nothing about it, though the effect on their currency earnings was a calamity. Writing about East-West trade, academician Oleg Bogomolov argues that it is necessary to improve the commodity pattern of East-West trade. He shows that fuels, raw materials, and food still predominate in the CMEA's exports to the West, accounting for 75 percent, while the proportion of manufactured goods constitutes only 25 percent and machines and equipment account for a mere 7 percent.[14]

The situation does not look much brighter in trade with the Third World, although the political interests here are obvious. According to Soviet figures, trade with developing countries grew from 7.8 percent of Soviet trade in 1960 to 13.5 percent in 1970, but declined to 12.7 percent by 1980.[15]

Looking at it from the other side, UNCTAD (United Nations Conference for Trade and Development) reports show that throughout the sixties and seventies trade with the Soviet Union remained below 2 percent of the Third World's total trade, and in the eighties the percentage is declining. Actually, the growth in Soviet-LDC (Less Developed Countries) trade has failed to keep pace with the far more dynamic growth of Western trade in the Third World. In recent years, even some Marxist-Leninist regimes are showing increasing interest in developing economic relations with the West (e.g., Mozambique and Tanzania). In short, the position of socialist countries in the world economy is such that fluctuations on the world market seriously affect them. Andre Gunder Frank noted that during the Great Depression afflicting capitalism in the early thirties the Soviets and Communist parties elsewhere were banking on aggravation of the crisis; today no socialist country seriously proposes to use the crisis of capitalism in order to destroy capitalism, as Lenin anticipated. They hope that the "crisis of capitalism will soon be over so that we can get back to business as usual."[16]

The path of Soviet industrialization has always followed one step behind Western technological progress, epitomizing its dependence on technological transfer from the more informational and computerized capitalist core. Moreover, in recent years the USSR has been compelled to import tens of millions of tons of grain from the United States and other capitalist countries to feed its population.

This is not only an economic issue, for at the end of the twentieth century there can be no strong ideological influence from a second-rate technological base. The importance of the technological asset in world power competition today is so great that its possession allows the United States to overcome the animosity generated by its domineering policies and to exercise a powerful attraction even among nations subject to such policies. Apparently the promise of technological breakthroughs involved in Reagan's Strategic Defense Initiative (SDI) is playing a much more important role than its military aspects in determining the participation of Western governments and corporations. Therefore, it is a strategic must for the Soviet Union to initiate a radical reform that will put it back in the world economic and technological race.

To conclude this point, I submit that if strategic pressures to modernize and update the economy did not exist, the conservatism of the party bureaucracy, thriving on the solid structures they have built into the system, could well withstand the forces of change.

IS CHANGE POSSIBLE IN THE EAST?

There is a widespread conviction among scholars and politicians that the Communist system is so petrified in its power structure that no significant political change is possible within it. This may sound paradoxical for a society that is in a transition period and is supposed to experience a continuous process of change. Indeed, Lenin taught us that under socialism political forms and institutions must continuously adapt to economic and social developments. Every Marxist will wholeheartedly agree.

But Stalin reversed that teaching, setting as the primary task the strengthening of the state and the widening of its role. Economic development was made dependent on the state plan, which became the alpha and omega of economic life. For each economic fact to occur a decision at the top was required, causing the economic system to lack a dynamic of its own. As a result, central political management of the economy has remained intact for five decades against the background of a revolution in science and technology that has transformed not only the character of productive forces but also the character of labor and of the social division of labor, including the culture and psychology of men and women.

The etatist direction given by Stalin to socialist ideology requires a thorough review. I refer to the switch from the working class to the state as the agent of change, from the masses to the leaders as the creators of history. The gist of this theoretical turnabout was cynically expressed by Stalin as he pointed out that the leadership of the state "passed fully and completely into the hands of one single party, into the hands of our party, which does not share and cannot share the ruling of the state with another party. This is what we call the dictatorship of the proletariat." Actually, the proletariat as such has no place in this definition except in the classic formula "dictatorship of the proletariat," which is being used here merely to identify it with the dictatorship of the party.

Moreover, as Branko Horvat rightly points out, although Marx meant class rule in his classic formula, in its Leninist-Stalinist interpretation the term has come to mean a dictatorial political regime; this has become the generally accepted meaning of the term in etatist countries and in the pseudo-Marxist literature.[17] To illustrate this, Horvat mentions the heading of a chapter in a book prepared by an academic institute in Moscow: "The Increase of the Ruling Role of the Communist Party in Society Is a Developmental Regularity of Democracy in Developed Socialism."[18]

Following the same line, the Soviet constitution of 1977, Article 20, declares, "In accordance with the communist ideal—the free development of each is the condition for the free development of all—the state pursues the aim of giving citizens more and more real opportunities to apply their creative energies, abilities, and talents and to develop their personalities in every way." In other words, everything comes from the state, which distributes rations of freedoms and opportunities as generous gifts. What has all this to do with Marx, who viewed the creative energies of people and the development of their personalities as on a collision course with the state whose main function is precisely to subject people to its domination, whether it is capitalist or socialist?

The absurdity of the etatist direction has become so obvious that in recent years an effort has been made to drown the whole issue in an idyllic ideological make-believe: "the state of all the people." What is the meaning of such a notion in a society that is still made up of classes?

For one thing, Marx thought that human emancipation and freedom would only be complete when people recognized and organized their own power as social power, so that they no longer would separate this social power from themselves as political power.[19] Political power is the dominating force embodied in the state, in any state machinery, whatever its class structure. Engels was even more specific in his famous letter to Bebel as he emphasized that because the state is but a temporary institution which is being used in struggle, in revolution, to repress adversaries by force, it is utter foolishness to talk about the free people's state: as long as the proletariat *still makes use* of the state, it uses the state not in the interest of freedom, but in order to repress adversaries, and once freedom becomes possible, the state as such ceases to exist.[20]

Lenin considered this statement as "one of the most outstanding, if not *the* most outstanding insights of Marx and Engels with regard to the theory of the state."[21] In other words, freedom is not and never has been the business of the state—which, by the way, was not created for freedom, and which possesses an entire mechanism that makes it totally unsuited for freedom. Rather than presenting the state as something wonderful, let us recognize that it is a necessary instrument for whatever domestic functions it must perform in the transition period and for external functions dictated by the existence of the interstate system.

Let me now turn to socialist democracy, probably the most ambiguous concept in the East European political vocabulary. The classic Marxist approach to this particular issue was formulated by Engels in 1891: "If one thing is certain it is that our Party and the working class can only come to power under the form of the democratic republic. This is even the specific form for the dictatorship of the proletariat."[22] Of course, Lenin could not go along with this; he simply replaced "democratic republic" with "republic of Soviets." The truth is that during the Revolution the Soviets constituted a democratic form of government in the sense that they were created by the masses, they debated publicly all the issues of the time, and their leaders were elected by secret ballot in strongly contested campaigns waged by the candidates. Later, however, the Soviets were stripped of power; under Stalin, the Bolshevik party's democratic norms and its practice of listening to clashing views before making decisions gave way to a rigid authoritarianism and pervasive militarization of life on every level. In the process, all the forms of popular power, from the Soviets to factory committees, were transformed into bureaucratic appendages of the central organ of power.

Having abolished every form of popular power, Stalin began to define Soviet democracy as a sort of mechanical result of the elimination of capitalists, boyards, and, implicitly, economic exploitation. He kept referring to a famous statement by Lenin to the effect that because of lack of exploitation the Soviet Union is a million times more democratic than the most advanced bourgeois country. Then he proceeded to theorize, presenting his political system as an organic component of a socialist society and establishing a sort of mechanical relationship between political system and social formation. It is extremely important to examine carefully such a theoretical claim, since its persistent reiteration throughout Eastern Europe purports to turn it into an absolute truth.

It is true that the abolition of property classes and of exploitation creates the premise for a more democratic society. The question, however, is whether the political system allows the citizens to take advantage of the potential for a more egalitarian economic society in terms of political power. Marx spoke often of the autonomy of politics vis-a-vis the economic base and even vis-a-vis classes. Thus, there is no automatic relationship between the two.

Beginning with ancient Greece, whose slave system formed both the democracy of Athens and the military dictatorship of Sparta, all social formations throughout history have afforded a diversity of political systems. Capitalism has tried the greatest variety of political systems—from the monarchical, presidential, and parliamentary pluralistic systems to military dictatorship and fascism—without challenging the ruling class and by keeping the bourgeoisie always in power, although not necessarily in its entire representation.

The only question that may arise is which political system serves better a particular social formation. It is this question that Stalin ordered taboo, and so have his successors. Nevertheless, this is precisely the question that is now coming to the fore in the USSR and Eastern Europe.

The Stalinist political system still prevailing throughout Eastern Europe has become the single greatest barrier to the further economic and social development of socialism. To the question whether this system best serves the cause of socialism and the working class, the answer is clearly negative. For the last twenty years the party bureaucracy running the socialist countries has been so absorbed with preserving its power over the economy that it has allowed Western capitalists to take advantage of the scientific-technological revolution and forge ahead in the economic competition. By doing so the political leaders of the West can rightly claim that they have well served the basic interests of their class. Obviously, the political leaders of the East cannot lay the same claim.

At the Twenty-seventh Congress, Mikhail Gorbachev criticized the Brezhnev leadership for bringing the Soviet economy to the point of stagnation. But what kind of political system allows such a poor performance to be curtailed only by death? Why should the development of the economy be made dependent on such leaders in a country that possesses the most numerous group of scientists and engineers in the world?

Lenin drew a clear distinction between government for the working people and government by the working people—the stage in which working people participate directly in making and carrying out decisions. As A. Butenko, a leading Soviet political scientist, put it recently, "Our society has not yet arrived at that stage." The new party program promises the instauration of socialist self-government; Butenko points out that the only objective criterion of self-government is "who holds the reins of power, to what extent the working people exercise power functions themselves, not by proxy, and in what areas of public life and to what extent they take the final decision."[23]

To better understand the workings of the present political system and its potential for change, a clear distinction should be made between leadership and apparat. As we must distinguish the state system from leadership in Western societies—the state system being the political instrument of class domination, while leadership provides for different conceptions about ways to use and direct state power—we must proceed similarly when dealing with the socialist political system. This analogy is based on the fact that as a rule those who hold the commanding positions in the state system (government and administration and its machinery, including the military and the coercive machinery) are recruited from the party apparat.

The apparat, far from being a social class, is nevertheless an observable, differentiated, interacting social stratum with sufficiently definite boundaries in Soviet society. Made up of full-time party officials and top people who run all state institutions, civil and military, it could well be described as the *ruling social group* in the USSR. Its members—the cadres—circulate constantly between managerial-technical jobs and party positions, participating regularly in party meetings and ideological indoctrination. The cohesive force of the group stems from the special social relations and status of its members, their position in the structure of power, their high salaries, and in particular the access they have to a wide range of restricted benefits and privileges—all combining to set this social elite apart from the rest of the population. The socio-political prerogatives are as important as economic ones in cementing the unity of the ruling bureaucracy. In 1980, total membership of this group (including central and local power) was estimated to be 250,000.

Whereas the apparat, like the state system, is programmed to follow the general direction of the domestic and foreign policy of the ruling class, the leadership is subject to virulent polemics and at times violent conflicts—beginning with Stalin, Trotsky, and Bukharin, through Malenkov to Khrushchev, and the troika of Brezhnev, Kosygin, and Podgorny. To put it in class terms, the apparat corresponds to the Leninist question of which class holds power, whereas the political conflict between various factions or leaders revolves around the question of who will exercise power on behalf of the ruling class: Stalin or Bukharin, the conservatives or the reformers, the moderates or the radicals, the hawks or the doves.

Therefore, in our analytical model, the apparat corresponds to the fundamental issue involving the class or bureaucracy in power; leadership concerns representation of that ruling class or group. That is why, on the basis of the general direction of policy, we may predict the position or behavior of the apparat on a particular issue; in the case of leadership, the situation is somewhat different because the autonomy the leadership enjoys allows for a variety of choices and behaviors in specific events or crises, making it hard to predict which will prevail. This is particularly valid as a new leader takes over and consolidates his own power base. Nobody was able to predict Stalin's evolution in the late twenties and early thirties or his initiative to approach Hitler and conclude the Molotov-Ribbentrop pact of 1939. Khrushchev was equally unpredictable, especially in foreign affairs; recall his insane idea to put missiles in Cuba. It is precisely that autonomy of leadership that has made it possible for significant shifts in policies in socialist countries–from Stalin to Khrushchev, from Mao to Deng Xiao Ping, from Novotny to Dubcek, from Rakocsi to Kadar.[24]

The question is, How much of an independent variable is a president, a chief of state, a leader? How much leverage does he have in domestic and foreign policy decisions, keeping in mind that international politics allows greater autonomy than domestic politics?

I suggest that leadership is not entirely an independent variable. We have seen in the case of Khrushchev what happened when his policies and initiatives came into conflict with the vested interests of the apparat; and we have noted that even

Kosygin's moderate reforms were sabotaged by the apparat and eventually nullified by those in the Politburo who aligned themselves with the apparat. More recently, it was Brezhnev's turn when, confronted with a sluggish economy that was rapidly approaching zero growth, he initiated some very mild measures to relax the heavy-handed planning system. In his blunt November 1981 report to the Central Committee plenary meeting, he complained that those measures "had not been resolutely implemented." Now who can do this kind of thing in the USSR, if not the apparat?

Indeed, the state system and, by analogy, the apparat acts as a strong conservative force. We are reminded that, whereas Harry Truman enjoyed the full cooperation of the state machinery when he altered toward the right the U.S. policy concerning the Soviet Union; the reaction of the same machinery was different when John F. Kennedy decided to abandon the perilous course of Cold War confrontation with the USSR. Walter Lippmann noted then that "there are strong bureaucratic interests in the Department of State, CIA and Pentagon which are opposed to change in policy by President Kennedy the same way as were the French generals in Algeria opposed to the change made by General deGaulle."[25]

The conclusion to be drawn is that the Soviet leadership could easily proceed with measures that suit the interests and ideological outlook of the apparat; when, however, a new strong leader tries to initiate structural changes that may affect the prerogatives of the apparat, he will be able to carry them out successfully only when a dislocation in the power structure has occurred (a change of guard in the Kremlin) that results in a split in the apparat of such magnitude that those in favor of change will get the upper hand. The cases of Kadar in Hungary and Deng Xiao Ping in China illustrate the working of that political mechanism.

Now we come to another theoretical point: Neither the apparat nor the leadership constitutes a monolithic bloc. There are various interests, tendencies, and viewpoints in the huge bureaucratic machinery that rules the USSR, and in particular there is an apparent generation gap that has developed lately, and it is only natural that these cleavages—however hidden and muted under normal conditions—be reflected at the top.

What is the significance of a new generation coming to power in the USSR and the possibility of change in the Soviet system deriving from it? The death of Leonid Brezhnev marked the end of an era in Soviet history. Indeed, the Twenty-sixth Congress of the Communist party, in 1981, was the last one dominated by the old guard of professional revolutionaries who were born and brought up in the traumatic years of the revolution and civil war followed by Stalin's social warfare, repression, and terror. While postrevolutionary Russia had been encircled by the White Armies and by the intervention of fourteen capitalist states bound to suppress the Revolution, the decades of rapid industrialization and forced collectivization under Stalin's rule unfolded in a hostile international environment of capitalist encirclement, economic embargo, and pressure designed to strangle and suffocate the young Soviet republic. Therefore, the habits of mind and styles of action characteristic of those hard times—revolutionary voluntarism, readiness to resort to coercion, and summary justice, in brief, anything required to get things done quickly and effectively—lingers on in the spirit of a whole generation of Communist leaders.

Precisely because the old guard saw its own end coming, it stubbornly clung to power. Something without precedent happened at the 1981 Congress: a fundamental Leninist principle requiring a Congress to elect a leadership reflecting in fair proportion the experience of the old and the innovative spirit of the young was grossly violated. Brezhnev and his associates dictated the reelection of the Politburo exactly in its old format, barring newcomers from the supreme organ of power at a time when the average age in the Politburo was 70.

Apparently, the old guard does not trust the new generation to think and act like them. And they are probably right. Persons born between the first Russian Revolution (1905) and that of 1917 (the Brezhnev generation) joined the party in the late 1920s and 1930s; most of them went to transitory-type colleges (chiefly engineering institutes), which were created especially for workers and low-level political activists, or took evening courses in the social sciences and economics. Since the great Stalinist purges of 1937-38 left many vacancies in party and state jobs, the people of the Brezhnev generation experienced unusually rapid promotions. As for the remaining contingents of that generation (born after the Revolution up to 1930), they were in their 20s when the war broke out—the age group most critically affected by the war not only because of the high proportion of wartime deaths, but because their studies had been disrupted and the chances of the survivors to obtain a college education in those years of destruction and administrative chaos were very slim.

It was not until the generation born in the 1930s came of age that a classic pattern of graduation became possible for political activists—from high school, direct entry into a full-time college, and normal graduation. Indeed, its members spent World War II in secondary schools and received their college education in the 1950s, when admissions standards became quite rigorous and programs very demanding. Hence, the new generation includes in fact the first contingents of political activists with a solid college education. The younger generation, now in their 50s, spent most of their formative years as political activists in the postwar years when the Soviet Union emerged as a world power with a political and military status equaled only by that of the United States. Although the unifying conformist pressure of political education and ideological indoctrination in the party is very strong, the postwar environment in which the new generation made its way into political life is so distinct that it could hardly fail to leave its mark on the new political contingents.

If my analysis is correct, it logically follows that the succeeding generation is riding the wave of the future and, therefore, we would expect a new party leader seeking a political base to gain position, regardless of age, as their representative. Indeed, the moment Yuri Andropov joined the Politburo he began signaling in that direction. What are the distinctive features of the new generation in terms of issues?

To begin with, the Soviet Union now is a modern industrial nation dominated by an educated working class and a huge detachment of scientists, engineers, and managers; therefore, it cannot be run the same way as was postrevolutionary backward Russia, with its archaic agriculture and mostly illiterate peasantry. This is where the two generations part ways, for the simple reason that one is emotionally attached and professionally accustomed to the old ways and the other is not.

The gap gets wider as we consider the serious problems besetting the Soviet Union today. Of course, as a new leadership takes power in the Kremlin, the logic of politics compels the ambitious successors of Brezhnev to provide an alternative to the stagnant society and sluggish economy that characterized the state of the Soviet Union from the seventies to the early eighties. Gorbachev's Report to the Congress presents precisely such an alternative. The promise of a radical reform in the economy is coupled with the realization that the "acceleration of society's development is inconceivable and impossible without a further development of all the aspects and manifestations of socialist democracy."

The Chernobyl accident has forcefully brought to the fore one vital aspect of democracy—an open information policy. Political scientists know that governments everywhere try to suppress embarrassing information; manipulation of information is not a Soviet monopoly. From glowing economic reports released by authorities just before elections through the famous "missile gap" concocted by the U.S. administration in the fifties (which proved a big hoax), public opinion in the

West has been subjected permanently to various "administered news." Nevertheless, vigorous independent sources and newspapers in the West more often than not succeed in exposing a government penchant for secrecy and good image. Watergate remains a classic.

In the USSR, secrecy and news control are rooted in czarist tradition as part of autocratic rule. "The czar knows best" has merely been replaced by "the Politburo knows best." Actually, nothing in the memory of Soviet society might evoke democratic procedures from below as a possible way of correcting the optimistic version of facts and figures provided by officialdom. Conversely, the belief that politics is simply tantamount to political initiatives and decisions from above is deeply embedded in Soviet society.

Now the scientific-technological revolution is forcing a change, and not only in the economy. The political system, with all power and initiative concentrated at the top, is coming into conflict with the revolution in computers and telecommunication. In a world in which communication is global and information instantaneous, the very assumption that information can be exclusively managed by a government is completely anachronistic and, as the Chernobyl accident abundantly shows, counterproductive. Such new instruments as computers, photocopiers, and word processors are simply incompatible with information and data dissemination control. The Soviets may renounce these only at the risk of long-term laggardness.

THE FORBIDDEN ISSUE IN THE EAST: POLITICAL REFORM

Why is political change the most sensitive item on the list of taboos in the East, so that a Marxist political scientist can write about it only abroad? Surely, this is too serious a problem to be left to the students rioting in Shanghai or in Kazakhstan.

At a time when the leaders of China are startling the world with their radical pronouncements on economic and cultural reforms and in the USSR shortcomings in the economy and cultural life are criticized with unprecedented candor, no serious debate is taking place on the political system, which in the last analysis is responsible for both the economic and cultural crises besetting these great nations.

Surely, the general talk about the urgency of democratization is not enough. One must deal with the criticial issues of political change, and these are not open for discussion.

The reason is that unlike the controversies on the economic and cultural situation, a thorough examination of the political process and decision-making must ultimately deal with the role and structure of the Communist party. Here the incongruence is not only between ideological tenets and political reality, but is something much more sensitive—between the actual norms and practices of the Communist party and its basic principles defined in the Party Rules (Statute), whose strict observance is obligatory for every member joining the party. Nowhere has Stalin's distortion of socialist principles been so blatant as in the way he molded the party and organized its activities. And, of course, those who exercise power on that basis find it hard to discuss or even listen to comments about such matters.

Recent developments have shown, however, that the vacuum of political ideas due to the lack of discussion is driving students and even academics to fill the vacuum with Western political values. A typical example is the controversial Manifesto smuggled from the USSR and published in the British paper *Guardian*—controversial both with regard to the identity of its authors and the position they take on political reform in the USSR. The Manifesto starts with a thorough and competent analysis of the outdated Soviet economic system and concludes that the country is threatened with becoming relatively underdeveloped in the world economy. To avoid this, the authors propose the following political changes: (1) press freedom; (2) a stop to persecution of people for their religious and political beliefs and a guaranteed freedom of speech; and (3) constitutional conditions for the creation of alternative political organizations (*Guardian*, 20 July 1986).

The paper maintains that among the authors of the Manifesto there are "party and government officials of high rank." But these people are professional politicians who surely know that the simple proclamation of press and speech freedoms amounts to nothing in the USSR. The Soviet constitution already provides for such freedoms and even pretends to guarantee them. Here is the biggest hoax in constitutional history. Hence, the document offers little in the way of a serious socialist alternative to the current Soviet system other than calling for the transplantation in a hostile environment of what are considered superior Western political values and methods.

The point is that to democratize and modernize a political system so deeply entrenched in the economic and social fabric of Soviet society, we must get rid of the ideological verbiage that confuses the issue and we must strike at the very core of the power structure. Only then can freedom of speech and of the press, including respect for human rights, flow naturally from the new political structures. In other words, reforming the political system requires first and foremost reforming the Communist party.

Now let us deal with the major aspects of an alternative political system: representation and the one-party system; bureaucracy and decision making; organization and distribution of power; and election of executive, legislative, and judiciary branches of government.

Representation and One-Party System

Because of historical circumstances and political traditions, including socialist ones, the adequate form for a democratic and fairly representative political system in the East is *party pluralism*, rather than a multi-party system.

Party pluralism means renouncing the monolithic concept of organization and transforming the Communist party into a representative political organization encompassing representatives of all social classes and major groups remaining in socialist society. Let us recall that the peasantry and the intellectuals have never been duly represented in the Bolshevik party, a fact that resulted in the forced collectivization, mass deportation, and killing of peasants and the massive repression of the intelligentsia without an effective resistance against such large-scale crimes within the party.

To acquire political legitimacy, the one-party system must guarantee all the social forces it claims to represent every opportunity to defend their specific interests and to express their different views. Otherwise, the emergence of alternative political parties is inevitable and perfectly legitimate.

The 1921 resolution forbidding the existence of factions in the Bolshevik party must be abolished. That resolution has eventually terminated debates on policy and economic issues and the practice of listening to clashing views before making final decisions within the party, thus suppressing inner party democracy. The consequence has been the formation of an oligarchic bureaucratic party structure that feels no need to consult party members or give them any opportunity to speak their minds and participate in decisions. Stalin cynically called this "military democracy," meaning that party members were merely expected to carry out orders from above. Although his brutal methods and excesses have been eliminated, military discipline and the interdiction to express dissenting views have remained in force.

In short, the acceptance of groups and factions within the Communist party is the fundamental principle of party democracy. And democracy in socialist society begins with democracy in the party. The Communist party can function as the leading political force in society only if it offers the component parts of that society full opportunity to express their views in the only party that exists.

The blunt truth is that ever since factions have been forbidden, the result has been that one faction (Stalin's, Khrushchev's, or Brezhnev's) has invariably run the party by eliminating the others. The same thing happened in China, where Mao eliminated Liu Shao Tsi and twice demoted Deng Xiao Ping in order to impose his policies. Innumerable are the names of brave and honest Communist leaders who were executed in the name of the dreadful monolithic concept. In fact, the interdiction of factions brought the law of the jungle to the Communist parties, as was so tragically illustrated by the Grenada case, where one faction murdered the leader of the other, thus inviting the U.S. intervention. How can we expect the tiny Afghan Communist party to broaden its political base, bringing the mujahedeem into the government, when the two factions in the party keep fighting and killing each other?

The monolithic concept of the Communist party must be discarded once and for all. In it lies the origin of the intolerant, narrow-minded, and repressive nature of the Communist party, the origin of the rule that practically suffocates the normal political and ideological life of the party.

The legalization of factions, including their fair representation in the Central Committee, should begin with the publication and critical examination of the works of Stalin, Trotsky, and Bukharin, without which the Revolution and the Bolshevik party itself are denied their history.

Bureaucracy and Decision Making

The Party Rules establish that the supreme organ of the party is the Congress, and in-between Congresses the Central Committee; both are elected by secret ballot. Until 1928-29, vivid debates on policy issues used to take place in those large forums and conflicting views could be expressed before final decisions were made—all reported publicly in the press. As Stalin consolidated his power and eliminated the leaders holding different views, the center of discussion and decision making was removed to the top hierarchical organs of the party bureaucracy—the Politburo and Secretariat; the discussion acquired a covert nature, with all major decisions being prepared in great secrecy in the latter organs, both led by the secretary-general.

Moreover, the list of delegates to the Party Congress as well as the list of candidates for the Central Committee have been drawn since by the central apparatus under the supervision of the Secretariat. I was elected three times as a delegate to the Congress, each time in a different region where very few people knew about my activities. The mechanism works so perfectly that at the 1981 Party Congress in Moscow all members of the Politburo were reelected, although their average age was 71, some of them ailing and having had one or two strokes.

In short, the removal of the center of decision making from the elected and deliberative bodies to the top bureaucratic organs has led to the bureaucratization of the Communist party. The Congress and the Central Committee became merely rubber-stamp bodies that are convened merely to endorse decisions already made by the Politburo. The most effective method to stifle discussion is to start the meetings of the Congress or Central Committee with a statement by the secretary-general. Who would dare take issue with the leader of the party? (Politburo member Boris Eltsin, who now runs Moscow, admitted to have praised Brezhnev's report in 1981 because he could not do otherwise).

At the February 1986 Congress, after Gorbachev's five-hour report, comrade Lev A. Kulidzanov went to the podium and said: "I whole-heartedly agree with his profound analysis and I felt deep regret that he had finished. Thank you, Mikhail

Sergeyevich, for your brilliant lesson." At this point, Gorbachev intervened: "Let us stop bowing to Mikhail Sergeyevich Gorbachev." But what else could Kulidzanov do than to approve the report and praise the author? The fact is that not one single speaker at the Congress dared to take issue with either the theoretical or the practical directives in Gorbachev's speech, though some of them are disputable or clearly inadequate. Why all the trouble to mobilize party organizations throughout the USSR and to bring thousands of delegates to the Congress and keep them busy for a week or so if they can contribute nothing to the decisions affecting the whole nation?

Probably the most striking illustration of this exercise in futility is the Twenty-second Congress of the CPSU in 1961, which adopted unanimously the program for the building of a Communist society in the USSR. It said that in the period 1961-70 the Soviet Union would "surpass the USA in per capita production"; in 1971-80 it would leave the United States far behind in industrial output and labor productivity; and grain output would reach 300 million tons annually. In addition, the demand for consumer goods would be fully satisfied, each family would have an apartment, rent would be gratis, and lunch in factories and schools would be free. In short, the Soviet people would live under communism. Alas, we are now in the mid-eighties and those goals are as far away as ever. Conversely, the gap between the United States and the USSR has widened in all the areas mentioned above, and the Soviets are importing more grains than in the sixties.

Recently, Gorbachev dismissed the 1961 projections as "groundless fantasies." But how was it possible that such fantasies initiated by the flamboyant Khrushchev could be approved, of course unanimously, by the Central Committee and the Congress? The answer is simple: All speakers kept bowing to Nikita Sergeyevich because this is what they were conditioned to do once the party leader had laid down the party line. I reread all the verbatim records of the postwar party

Congresses and could not find one single speaker making the slightest critical remark on the report of the secretary general.

Clearly, such a decision-making mechanism is antiscientific and error-prone. Modern scientific theory requires the presentation of at least two or three projects for discussion and the person who makes the final decision speaks at the end of the debate, after listening to the various opinions expressed in the respective meeting. If only one project is submitted for consideration, the outcome of the discussion is predetermined; in fact, no selection takes place, no arguments clash, and the course of action is already decided.

The Congress and Central Committee should be restored as the supreme deliberative and decision-making bodies of the party, with the Politburo and Secretariat reduced to organs in charge of implementing the decisions. Deliberations of the supreme bodies should take place on the basis of reports drafted by party commissions appointed by the Secretariat as independent units; neither the Secretariat nor the Politburo should interfere with the work of the commissions. The secretary-general should speak only at the end of the debates, after listening to various opinions and consulting the other members of the Politburo. The secretary-general's conclusive remarks will establish the party line and the final decision, which will be binding to all party members.

The report to be presented in Congress first should be distributed to all party organizations and widely discussed in their meetings. Resolutions of party organizations concerning the draft report should be hierarchically submitted and eventually summarized by the Secretariat as a co-report before the Congress. At the same time, opinions would be expressed in the media.

Every member of the party should be entitled to have his own opinions on the issues under debate and to express them freely. After the resolution of the Congress, all party members should abide by it and fight for its implementation.

Organization and Distribution of Power

The numerous crimes and acts of terror ordered by Stalin, the devastating cultural revolution initiated by Mao, the genocide carried out by Pol Pot, and the disastrous economic policies followed by Gierek all lead to the inevitable conclusion that the political system in the East fails to provide effective ways and means to check the abuse of power.

Historical experience will tell us that the best method to deal with potential abuse is the separation of power between the executive branch of government and the legislative and judicial institutions. Such separation could be established through the constitution and by organizing elections in such a way as to make offices in the legislative and judiciary branches independent of the executive. This is what is now required in the socialist countries.

In addition, the system of virtual life-peerage enjoyed by party leaders, regardless of their political performance, must be terminated. This has been the source of power abuse, personality cult, nepotism, above-the-law behavior, and corruption. Therefore:

- Members of the Central Committee should be elected by Congress for a maximum of four terms (sixteen years) and members of the Politburo and Secretariat for a maximum of two terms (eight years).
- Persons holding high positions in the party should not be allowed to occupy offices in the executive branch of government.

Election of Executive, Legislative, and Judicial Branches of Government

The transition from the present administrative electoral system to a democratic system will amount to an overhaul of the electoral process, which can be done only gradually. Therefore, a new electoral system first should be elaborated by jurists and then introduced experimentally at the local level, in villages and towns. Following are some principles for the new system:

1. Candidates should be nominated by citizens in well-established constituencies without interference from the central power organs.
2. Candidates should not be required to be members of the Communist party.
3. A minimum of two candidates should be nominated for each office.

In both China and the USSR the leadership is aware that radical changes will be required in their societies if socialism is to step into the twenty-first century. Both complain, however, that strong conservative forces within the party oppose change for different reasons.

To avoid a new "revolution from above" in the Stalinist style, the best way of dealing with the conservative forces is to give them a chance to get out of their hiding and openly express their views in the party and in the public at large. This is what democracy is all about. The reformist forces in the party thus will be mobilized to fight for a better future society, demonstrating whether their parties still have a revolutionary spirit and drive in the world of today.

Gorbachev's proposals advanced at the Central Committee meeting on 27 January 1987 constitute a step in the right direction. In fact, he advocates the democratization of the system to an extent without precedent in Communist history. Not only does he propose to allow citizens to nominate several candidates in elections, a measure already practiced in Hungary, but he suggests that even in the Communist party secretaries of local organizations up to the central committees in the union republics be elected by secret ballots with an unlimited number of candidates in the voting list. This is a significant shift that introduces the principle of accountability of Communist leaders to party members, making the election of leaders dependent on the way their performance and prestige are evaluated *below* by party members—a far cry from the present system in which both the nomination and appreciation of such leaders' performance are decided by the superior party organs. It is this top-to-bottom selection of local leaders that has generated bureaucratization and sycophancy toward the top leadership in the Communist parties. Moreover, Gorbachev pointed out that "the Politburo's opinion is that further democratization should also apply to the formation of the central leading bodies of the party," meaning the Politburo and the Secretariat. Of course these are just proposals, but even their theoretical formulation is of extraordinary importance. The evidence that this time Gorbachev has touched a sensitive nerve in the political system is the lack of publicity of his January speech throughout the East and in China.

Two Approaches to Reform: China and USSR

Recent political developments have brought to the fore the different approaches of China and the U.S.S.R. to reform. To better understand the nature of that difference, we must note first that China is lagging in terms of the historical stage of development, and, therefore, while systemic change in the USSR would take fifteen to twenty years, in China it would take at least fifty to sixty years. This is why in China economic change has been hasty, sweeping, and radical, beginning with the unleashing of market forces in agriculture. This suggests a more venturesome strategy appearing as a sort of steeplechase marked by rapid advances and sudden retreats or setbacks. In the USSR, although the rhetoric is revolutionary, the process of change is slow, cautious, and gradual, with every major decision being made only after experimenting on a local basis. The "industrial experiment" initiated in 1984 in five key ministries, was extended in 1985 to 12 percent, in 1986 to 50 percent, and only in 1987 to the entire industry.

With respect to intellectual freedoms and political democratization the difference between the two is even more apparent. Gorbachev has stated time and again that democratization is essential and rebuffed those who fear that democracy might disorganize society: "Democracy is not the opposite of order; it is order of a higher degree, not based on implicit obedience and mindless execution of instructions, but on full-fledged, active participation of all citizens in the affairs of society." And he concluded emphatically: "It is either democracy or social inertia and conservatism. There is no third way, comrades." (*Pravda*, 26 February 1987).

In China, the 1987 campaign against intellectual freedom and political dissent reveals a much more fundamental creed. The fact that the "people's democratic dictatorship" is among the four cardinal principles of modernization should remind us that while dictatorship of the proletariat meant class rule to Marx, Stalin interpreted the notion to mean a dictatorial political regime. That this is also Deng's interpretation was shown by his February 1987 Directives to party cadres which was brought to the attention of three Western correspondents by the Central Committee spokesman in Beijing. After praising Polish leaders for their firm attitude in the face of Solidarity's opposition, Deng concluded: "That shows clearly that if we don't use dictatorial methods, it won't do. We must not only talk about dictatorial methods, but also practice them."(*Washington Post*, 27 February 1987).

Apparently, while Gorbachev feels secure to advocate more democracy, having attracted the intelligentsia, the scientists, and engineers (totalling almost 15 million people) on the barricades of the reform, Deng Xiao Ping fears that the Chinese population (still beset by widespread illiteracy) is insufficiently prepared to withstand Western ideological influence. Moreover, the need to assimilate the computer and information revolution that plays such an important part in Gorbachev's campaign for democracy and openness, does not have the same urgency in China.

THE HIGH-TECH WORLD CONTEST

Four recent developments are but signals that the new round in the world economic contest for positions of dominance may well focus on high technology. In Western Europe, the project Eureka designed to give an impulse to joint research in high technology is being followed by a major effort of EEC members to turn their organization into a real common market large and powerful enough to face the American and Japanese advance in technology and world markets. In the East, the Soviet party Congress and the subsequent Congresses in Eastern Europe have all emphasized the urgency of dealing with the threat of a widening economic gap with the West, giving special importance to the Comprehensive Program of Scientific and Technological Progress adopted by the 1984 CMEA Summit for the next fifteen to twenty years, in which computers, microprocessors, robots, and biotechnology are listed as priorities. Ronald Reagan's SDI project is wooing industrial nations to join the research work with the promise of new breakthroughs in technology. Also, large U.S. and Japanese scientific working groups are engaged in a fierce race for the development of the fifth-generation computer.

Computer technology and microprocessors are pushing industries and society as a whole to a higher stage of efficiency and wealth while the new planetary communications already bestow upon the nations developing them economic and even, political power. From 1972 to 1985 the average annual growth of high-tech products has reached 7.6 percent in the United States, 14 percent in Japan, and less than 5 percent in Western Europe. In the East, electronics have developed at a rapid pace, about 6 percent, but other items of high technology are not even recorded in statistics. Apparently the spectacular achievements of the Soviets in outer space and the highly advanced technology of their weaponry had no effect on the civilian production process. As a result, in the same period, the share of high technology total exports rose in the United States from 29 percent to 38 percent, in Japan from 16 percent to 42 percent, and Western Europe's share remained the same as twenty years ago, 25 percent. East European exports of high technology are minimal.[26]

Japan emerges as the strongest contender for a predominant position in high technology. Lacking a heavy military sector to sap investment capital and scientific and managerial talent and enjoying high domestic savings and stable industrial relations, Japan is moving toward a position of global economic supremacy. Japan's exports are nearly double those of the Soviet Union and, if recent trends continue before 1990, Japan will supplant the United States as the world's leading trading power. The intrusion of Japanese high-tech products on the U.S. and West European markets is advancing at an alarming rate.

The United States, with its decline from half of the world gross product in 1950 to less than 25 percent in the eighties, is still the largest economic and financial power. In recent years enormous U.S. defense spending has led to mounting federal budget deficits and the dwindling competitiveness of its industrial and agricultural goods have created a growing deficit in its balance of trade. Not even the nearly 30 percent devaluation of the dollar could reverse those negative trends. However, the United States was and remains the principal innovator of technological know-how and the principal generator of new high-tech products in the world. The problem emphasized by U.S. economists is that higher capital costs keep driving investors to go overseas even in the high-tech industrial branches.

The rapid U.S. and Japanese advance in high technology has produced a strong reaction of self-defense and a tendency to close ranks in the two power centers most directly threatened by this economic thrust: Western Europe and Eastern Europe.

Because technology does not operate as a one-directional sweep but moves in a dual and contradictory way, we see in both regions a dialectical interplay between the forces working for integration and those trying to reassert selfish national interests.

In Western Europe we hear many voices arguing these days that only a single unified market could stand up to U.S. and Japanese competition. Businesspeople who once quietly enjoyed the benefits of protected markets in their own countries now are lobbying for a common market. Philips, the Dutch-based multinational company that is Europe's largest manufacturer of consumer electronics, estimates that it would have earned an extra $175 million last year (50 percent more profit) if it had been able to operate in a unified market. The maze of safety regulations and technical norms so different from one country to another complicate packing, labeling, warehousing, and shipping—each process costing money; the extra cost of border formalities and of various rates for national sales taxes amounts to $50 billion a year, according to the West European parliament.[27]

Moreover, most new electronic products require such a large investment that no single national market can repay it. A decade ago it cost about $50 million to develop an office switchboard with a twenty-year market life, but today the research and development of such a product would cost more than ten times that because of the microchips and software involved, and the market life would be halved. To recoup such an investment, a company needs sales of $10 billion to $15 billion in ten years, which not even the French and Italian markets together could absorb. With all its twelve members, the EEC could emerge as the world's largest affluent market with 320 million inhabitants, significantly larger than the United States with 234 million and Japan with 117 million.

On the other hand, West Europeans who oppose the plan to abolish frontier formalities are still strong; some governments would like a common market a la carte, choosing only the convenient part of it. West Germany, with its industrial power, stresses unhindered circulation of manufactured goods; France advocates a free unified market for its agricultural products; and Britain is ready for free competition in services in which its bankers and insurers, accountants, and consultants excel. But the typical manifestation of national resistance to market integration is the institution of PTT (Post, Telegraph, Telephone) existing in West European countries. At a time when telephones and computers are merging into a single technology in the sphere of planetary communications, PTT controls not only telephone networks but the transmissions they carry, the rates, the technical standard of equipment that can be attached to the networks, bulletin boards, and banking by phone. In the meantime, Japan has started work on a universal phone system capable of carrying together conversations and data flows, facsimile transmissions, and possibly television transmissions. Such a system is the key to the information society, says the head of the European community's Commission on Information Technology. But to build such a system West European countries would have to adopt uniform technologies to supplant the existing national systems. The PTTs resist this, and therefore nothing is being done.

Under such pressures, the twelve EEC members took a first step toward economic integration by curbing the Treaty of Rome provision requiring unanimity in decision making. From now on, a majority of members can impose a decision, and an EEC summit meeting is going to take up the issue of market unification.

Like the United States, the Soviet Union has devoted a large part of its gross national product to the military effort, reaching a position of parity with the United States. However, the price has been very high, exacting a heavy toll on living standards and diverting political energies from the sorely needed modernization of the economy. When Gorbachev criticizes the Brezhnev era he refers to the years when in the West a series of technological breakthroughs resulted in a considerable expansion of productive forces. But the truly crucial development that seems to have alarmed the new Soviet leadership is the advent of the so-called third industrial revolution involving the computerization of economic and social activities and the large-scale introduction of microelectronics and robots in the industrial process. Here the prospect of a serious technological lag compared to Western advances had become apparent. A series of special directives issued lately by the Central Committee and Politburo are urging such efforts as the production of automatic machinery and installation based on microchips, increased output of industrial robots, and production of various types of computers. A decision was made to begin the training of high school students on computers. Also, the 1984 summit of CMEA (Comecon) established a common program to develop scientific cooperation in view of expanding research and production in such areas as computers, microelectronics, and robots.

The crux of the matter, of course, is the outdated economic mechanism stubbornly maintained since the thirties. For the time being, the measures decided at the Soviet party Congress aim at improving the functioning of the system, which evidently is not enough. A radical restructuring is advocated by many economists to keep the economic mechanism abreast of technological innovation and to make it sufficiently flexible to adapt to rapid technological change. This goes, of course, for all Eastern countries suffering from the same institutional sclerosis. My point is that while domestic conditions may dictate a slow process of change, it seems increasingly obvious that the strategic position of the CMEA in the world economy will require a more rapid course in the transformation of the economic mechanism. Nothing looks more convincing in this respect than the situation of the USSR and its partners in the high-tech contest raging now on the world markets: They simply do not count in that race. It is only in outer space and in the military competition that the Soviet Union is a strong contender recognized as such by the whole world. But how long can the socialist economies survive facing a capitalist core that is becoming increasingly computerized and informational?

In this respect, we should note that the U.S. and Japanese advance in high technology has produced in Moscow and other Eastern capitals a strong tendency toward joining forces with Western Europe. For the first time, CMEA has officially recognized the institution of EEC and negotiations have been initiated to establish forms of cooperation between the two. An article in the authoritative Soviet monthly *International Affairs* (January 1986) is significantly entitled "The New Stage of the Scientific-Technological Revolution and East-West Economic Ties." The author, A. Bykov, draws a parallel between the vigorous efforts made in Western Europe to cope with the advance of the United States and Japan and the similar efforts made in Eastern Europe. His conclusion is startling: "A certain coordination of these processes within the framework of all-European division and cooperation of labour could yield undoubted advantages for the whole continent." The Soviet author goes as far as suggesting that joint ventures be set up to develop and introduce new technologies on an all-European scale. He suggests also an "organizational structure of relations between the CMEA and EEC" to direct cooperation through "the whole science-technology-production-marketing cycle." Ten years ago this would have been inconceivable. The fact is that the Soviets and their Eastern partners cannot reconcile themselves with being outsiders in the high-tech contest on the world markets. This may prove decisive in determining both the speed of domestic change and the opening to the world economy, particularly Western Europe.

THE EMERGENCE OF AN ALTERNATIVE STRATEGY FOR THE YEAR 2000

The beginning assumption of this forecast is that underlying the current debate on the relevance of Marxism today and economic reform in the socialist countries is the emergence of an alternative strategy within the world Communist movement. Although the new strategy originates in China, I feel that the urgency of a radical change in Soviet society advocated by the leadership in Moscow may turn the strategic choice into the central theoretical issue involving revolutionary forces around the world in years to come.

Historical Perspective

From the beginning, the first socialist state—the USSR—had to struggle for the attainment of two major strategic objectives: the fundamental *economic task of catching up with capitalism*, without which socialism could not assert itself as a superior socioeconomic system, and the *politico-military aim of acquiring a world posture* sufficiently strong to withstand the challenges from the hostile capitalist environment.

In the twenties and thirties, Stalin was obviously driven by the economic and strategic imperative of building a modern industrial base to overcome Russia's underdevelopment; at the same time, the capitalist encirclement made him equally concerned with forging armed forces capable of defending the conquests of the Revolution. Neither the economic assets nor the military capability at the time allowed the Soviet Union to play a major role in world politics.

It was only during World War II that conditions became propitious for the Soviet Union to enter the world power game. Initially, in his dealings with Hitler, Stalin began to learn the rules of the game. He discussed with Roosevelt and Churchill not only the strategy to defeat Hitlerite Germany but also the postwar political organization of the world.

After World War II, the USSR emerged as one of the two world protagonists, continually clashing with the United States for a hegemonial position, initially in Europe and eventually on all continents. As the revolutionary process extended into Eastern Europe under the umbrella of the Red Army, the United States countered with the containment policy, the North Atlantic Treaty Organization, and so on. The Cold War concentrated the emphasis in Soviet policy on the politico-military objective, despite the fact that the USSR badly needed to reconstruct its devastated economy. The success of socialist revolution through politico-military means in both Eastern Europe and China reinforced the belief that Communists were at their best in political organization and armed struggle. Generally, the conviction was growing that economic competition was less important than the territorial expansion of socialism.

This conviction culminated in the 1960 Moscow Statement of the Communist and Worker's Parties proclaiming that the content and direction of human society are determined principally by the world socialist system. The essential error in this statement stems from a gross underestimation of the *economic* factor, which for a Marxist is in the last analysis decisive in society's development. The gap between the rich nations and the poor continued to widen; the international division of labor operated in favor of the capitalist industrial nations; and the socialist countries lagged behind the capitalists in all major economic indicators. Such a world could not be described as being determined in content and direction by socialism. The reverse seemed more congruent with reality, as we have already amply documented in this book.

For a while Khrushchev seemed concerned more with the fundamental economic task of catching up with capitalism. To relax the heavy burden of military expenditures on the economy he made his spectacular proposal for general and complete disarmament. But nothing came of that.

In the early seventies the policy of detente offered another opportunity for a review of priorities in Soviet strategy. The basic document of detente, the Nixon-Brezhnev accord, was essentially a package deal in which politico-military matters were lumped together with trade-technological commitments in a quid pro quo system. Apparently the Soviets were chiefly interested in the trade-technological end of the bargain while the United States viewed it as an instrument for securing a worldwide status quo in political and military terms. A U.S. author noted: "Trade, credits, and technology transfers, it was thought, could be exchanged for Moscow's agreement to put a lid on the strategic arms race, to cooperate in managing crises in the third world, and most immediately to help the United States extricate itself gracefully from Vietnam."[28] Indeed the Soviet leadership was led to expect economic and technological benefits that could allow the USSR to make significant headway in economic competition. Informed sources at that time disclosed that Henry Kissinger had mentioned a $10 billion target for the U.S.-Soviet volume of trade. It was on that understanding that the Soviets accepted the key sentence of the agreement, which stated that it would be contrary to the objectives of detente if one of the parties would seek to obtain advantages (read: expand its sphere of influence), whether direct or indirect, to the detriment of the other. From the American viewpoint, this was a pledge to maintain stability along the periphery (in the southern continents) as a condition for a stable peace at the center.

However, the two amendments to the trade bill adopted in 1974 by the U.S. Senate (linking trade to Soviet emigration policy and setting a low ceiling on credits) were viewed in Moscow as measures that canceled the most attractive part of the deal. Kissinger, the architect of the trade-off in the deal, tried in vain to convince the Senate to drop the amendments.

Thus, the Soviets felt free to help Angola and Ethiopia with weapons, actions that were perceived in Washington as canceling the remaining part of the agreement. President Carter's campaign on human rights directed against the Soviets added insult to injury. As an epilogue, the failure of the U.S. Senate to ratify SALT II marked the funeral of detente. Thus, when the Soviets decided to act in Afghanistan there was nothing left of the package deal. Obviously, the emphasis in Soviet strategy switched again to the politico-military buildup. In official documents, the success of socialism was measured in terms of territorial extension rather than in terms of economic performance. The USSR built its military forces to the point of becoming a global world power, having the capability to project its forces on any point of the globe, a fact that influenced its foreign policy.

Therefore, Gorbachev's critique of Brezhnev's failure to act on the economic front implicitly raises the question of priorities in Soviet strategy. This very question is being pushed on the agenda by a sober appraisal of the state of affairs in all three subsystems of our world: (1) the socialist countries are losing the economic-technological competition with the West and the East-West gap is getting wider; (2) in the West at a time when the capitalist economy is going through a protracted crisis, with high unemployment as the main casualty, the Communist parties are losing ground; and (3) in the Third World, Marxist-Leninist regimes are facing economic problems that seem insurmountable while a series of countries in the Pacific and Southeast Asia following the capitalist way of development enjoy high rates of economic growth and rapid industrialization.

There must be something wrong with a strategy that provides neither the prospect of winning the competition nor the chance of taking advantage of favorable circumstances. What else is a strategy for?

The Choice of Strategy

Why have the Soviets and other Communist governments chosen to rely on politico-military means in their strategy against capitalism rather than on economic performance?

In the world economy, as already shown, the socialist states hold an inferior position; they are thus subject to an unequal exchange in their trade with the West, resulting in a large foreign debt and heavy interest payments to Western banks and governments. In the politico-military sphere, however, the USSR and its allies have succeeded in recent decades to build a force equal to that of the United States and its allies. This allows the USSR to display political and military initiative on the world scene that may affect, for better or for worse, the international political climate. The Soviets surely could do nothing of that sort in the world economy, where their actions are adaptive rather than disruptive. The emphasis on politico-military means seems simply to have been a more convenient choice of strategy.

The trouble is that in times of peace it is the economic factor that takes precedence. Nothing better illustrates this point than the cases of Vietnam and Ethiopia. The heroic military victory of the Vietnamese over the American interventionists was expected by most analysts to have a tremendous impact in the whole region in favor of socialism. But soon a wholly different situation developed. As the Communist leadership in Hanoi passed to peaceful constructive activity, the economy went from bad to worse and even the few modern installations left by the Americans in Saigon were crippled by Hanoi's ineptitude and mismanagement. Now who in the world would want to emulate such a model?

Turning their backs on the economy, Hanoi leaders decided to focus on what they knew best: in 1979 approximately 200,000 Vietnamese troops invaded Cambodia with Soviet support, and they have been there ever since.

In ten years of a Marxist-Leninist regime, the Ethiopian leader Mengistu, well supplied with weapons from the Soviets, distinguished himself by waging fierce battles against Somalia and the Eritrean Liberation Front (both claiming pro-socialist orientation) only to discover that the country was completely unprepared when it was struck by a devastating drought and famine. We should add here that the same focus on politico-military means drove the Soviets to send their troops into Afghanistan. In all these cases, the underestimation of the economic factor is apparent. In the meantime, South Korea, Taiwan, Singapore, and Hong Kong, beating the world records of economic growth, became showcases for the capitalist method of development in the Third World.

This kind of comparative study equally applies to the political impact of the East on the West. With the image of "real socialism" marred by lagging technology, food shortages, and shabby consumer goods, how could we expect working people in the West to fight for socialism? Although quite a few are disenchanted with capitalism and would like to see radical changes in the socioeconomic structure, the socialist model offered by the East is not very appealing. The artists and intellectuals of the West that were strongly attracted by the noble ideals of socialism are increasingly disappointed by the lack of democracy in the Eastern model. This model is in fact a political nuisance to the anti-capitalist forces in the West and we can understand why some of them, particularly the Italian communists, are disassociating themselves from it. Therefore, the issue of reform in socialist countries is dialectically linked with that of strategy of the Communist movement.

Yuri Andropov, who initiated the process of economic change in the USSR, and more recently Mikhail Gorbachev, a declared advocate of a radical reform, both have introduced their cases in favor of change by recalling Lenin's teaching that the Soviet Union should exert its influence on other countries mainly through its economic policy and the level and direction of its socioeconomic development.[29] Deng Xiao Ping stated on 7 January 1985 that China's output will quadruple by the end of the century, and as a result China's influence in world affairs will be much greater.

There is a certain logic in statements that link economic reform with the world impact of nations' policies and well-being. This is in fact the crux of the strategic choice. We live in the world of the nuclear era when the use of force has ceased to be the decisive factor in changing power relations in world politics. Moreover, a significant change has occurred in the dynamics of power itself in the sense that the relative weight of the military component of power has been reduced in proportion to the role of economic, financial, and technological components. Western Europe and Japan have become world power centers, though neither possesses a significant independent military force commensurate with that position.

This is not to say that military strength will be eliminated from the attributes of power. Despite its setbacks and the severe limitations imposed on the use of force, military strength and its manifestation, the use of force, is here to stay. The fact is that the insane nuclear race and the increasingly exorbitant military expenditures have not been affected by the latest developments. Military powers, particularly superpowers, are trying to maximize the impact of their nuclear superiority in order to improve their relative posture in the economic and technological war.

Nevertheless, the actual shift in the dynamics of power and the virtual veto on the use of nuclear force make the world power constellation increasingly dependent on economic and technological performance. It may take some time for political institutions and leaders to grasp that new reality and adapt to it. The leadership of China is probably the first to have grasped it, making the boldest turnabout in modern history from military build-up to an economic drive for modernization. We could mention quite a few domestic motivations to explain that cardinal shift in policy, but I venture to suggest that strategic considerations were paramount. The fact is that with command-type planning providing a snail-paced tempo of economic development, China could never hope to acquire in the world power game a competitive position commensurate to its size. Recall that by the end of the seventies Taiwan's exports were greater than China's. Something drastic had to be done to put China on the world economic map, and Deng Xiao Ping did it.

Although the Soviets do not have to start from scratch, their case is much more complicated. The USSR is a global world power with strategic objectives very much on the mind of its leadership; in this respect, Moscow is engaged in a fierce politico-military competition with Washington in which its formidable military force constitutes its main asset. What is more, the Soviet nuclear umbrella plays a major role in cementing the unity of Warsaw Pact members. A shift from military buildup to economic competition is therefore harder to make in Moscow.

The Soviet leaders, however, cannot reconcile themselves to the prospect of the Soviet Union falling further behind in the world economic competition. The bold and radical measures proposed by Gorbachev for nuclear and conventional disarmament point in the right direction: stopping the arms race is a prerequisite for an all-out Soviet effort in the economic contest.

A New World Power Constellation by the Year 2000?

Right now the most alarming threat comes from Western capitalism. The United States is far ahead and the historical task of overtaking it economically seems a hopeless proposition in Moscow. Japan's exports are nearly double those of the Soviet Union and its gross national product may soon surpass that of the USSR, although Japan's population is less than half that of the Soviet Union.

But a different type of challenge is coming from the other end of the spectrum—China. In a very short time, the freeing of market forces in agriculture resulted in a record 400 million tons of grain crops in 1984, making China a grain exporter. Industrial growth in 1985 reached 17.7 percent, the highest in the world. Approximately 1,800 foreign companies attracted to the huge Chinese market began joint ventures with Chinese enterprises, investing billions of dollars and bringing in the most modern technology. The problem for Beijing now is how to moderate that impetuous surge and keep the process under control. Most observers now are convinced that Deng's goal of quadrupling the gross annual value of industrial and agricultural production by the year 2000 should be taken seriously. China's main asset as a world power is the size of its population. If its billion people become a modern productive force the world power constellation will look differently, as shown in Table 7. Long-term projections must take into account an extended base period. However, I have chosen 1980-85 in the table because in those years certain salient trends for the future development of the world powers took shape (the United States' and Japan's advance in high tech-

Table 7.
Ranking in the World Economy

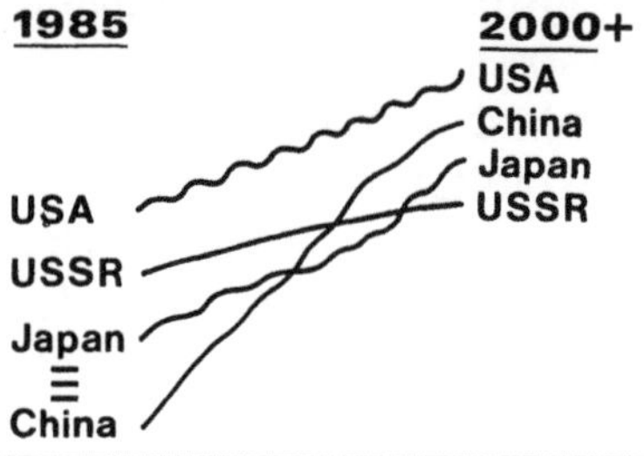

nology, China's economic reform, and the USSR's industrial experiment). The projection to the year 2010 is calculated on the assumption that GNP will, on average, increase by the growth rate of the base period. The Soviet Union faces the prospect of being pushed back to fourth place in the world economy, behind the United States, China, and Japan.

China's New Strategy and the Future

To consolidate the shift from strategy based on politico-military factors to one emphasizing economic performance, China has adopted along with its radical economic reform the principle of *one state, two systems*. This means that while continental China will develop its socialist system, Hong Kong and Taiwan will retain their capitalist system and way of life for 50 years or so, yet they will belong to one state, China. The idea behind this principle is that the population in Hong Kong and Taiwan enjoy a much higher standard of living and therefore it would be wrong and counterproductive, as Deng puts it, to conquer the two by force and destroy their prosperity. For the first time in history a Communist leader in power has acknowledged publicly that because of historical conditions sections of its people are better off under capitalism and the only rational solution is to work hard and patiently to bring the entire nation to the same high level of development and prosperity.

Clearly, this principle can be applied to the world scene in which, due to the historical condition that socialism began in less-developed countries, the populations in Western societies enjoy a higher standard of living despite the shortcomings of capitalism—from exploitation and glaring inequalities to recessions, inflation, and unemployment. The rational solution is not the territorial expansion of underdeveloped socialism by politico-military means but the construction of an efficient economic system that can bring a higher standard of living to the citizens of socialist countries.

China is gradually emerging as the champion of a new strategy based primarily on economic success and popular well-being. If the urban reform produces the same result as the rural reform, the new strategy is bound to acquire a tremendous following, particularly in the Third World. The Kremlin then will be confronted with a dramatic choice: to cling to the old ways and rely increasingly on military power to exert its international influence, or to proceed with a radical change in both economic policy and global strategy. The issue of leadership in the Communist movement will depend on that choice. In fact, the future of the world will depend on that choice.

NOTES

1. *Programul Partidului Communist al Uniunii Sovietice* (Bucharest: Editura Politica, 1961).
2. Karl Marx, *Capitalul*, v. 1 (Bucharest: Ed. P.M.R., 1948), 187; and *Mizeria Filofozofiei* (Bucharest: Ed. P.C.R., 1947), 97.
3. Lenin, *Opere*, v. 26 (Bucharest: Editura Politica, 1964), 72.
4. *Historical Materialism*, F. V. Constantinov, ed. (Bucharest: Editura Literatura Politica, 1952), 651.
5. N. Khrushchev, *On the Program of the CPSU* (Bucharest: Editura Politica, 1962), 180.
6. "The Program of the CPSU," *New Times*, Moscow, 31 March 1986, 28.
7. Ibid., 22.
8. Ibid., 28.
9. Mikhail Gorbachev, "Political Report of the CPSU Central Committee to the 27th Congress," *New Times*, Moscow, 10 March 1986, 24.
10. Mikhail Gorbachev, op. cit., p. 26.
11. Ibid., 26.
12. Ibid., 26.
13. *Pravda*, 29 March 1986.
14. O. Bogomolov, "Prospects for Economic Cooperation," *New Times*, Moscow, No. 8 (February 1986).

15. *SSSR Tsentral'noe Statisticheskoe Upravlenia* (Moscow: 1972), 491; and 1981, 537.

16. Andre Gunder Frank, "The Political Challenges of Socialism" (Paper delivered at Round Table, Dubrovnik, 1985).

17. Branko Horvat, *The Political Economy of Socialism* (Armonk, N.Y.: Sharpe, 1982), 287.

18. Ibid., 465.

19. K. Marx, *Opere*, vol. 9 (Bucharest: Editura Politica, 1964); see also *Werke*, vol. 6 (Stuttgart: 1962), 795.

20. Friedrich Engels, Appendix to *Critique of the Gotha Program* (Bucharest: Ed. P.M.R., 1948), 116-17.

22. K. Marx and F. Engels, *Correspondence 1846-1895* (New York: International Publishers, 1935), 486.

23. Anatoly Butenko, "From the Dictatorship of the Proletariat to Socialist Government," *New Times*, Moscow, no. 8 (February 1986).

24. For readers interested in pursuing the study of the social pyramid and of the political structures characteristic of Soviet society, a very rich literature is available. Some pertinent data substantiating the official doctrine can be found in the following studies: N. A. Barsukov and I. N. Yudin, *Sotsial'naya baza KPSS* (Moscow, 1967), dealing with the social basis of the Communist party of the Soviet Union; E. B. Barabashev and K. F. Sheremet, *Sovetskve gosudarstvo i obshchestvennost v usloviakh razvernutogo stroitelstva kommunisma* (Moscow, 1962), which presents the relationship between the state and society and how it has evolved in the process of socialist construction; F. M. Burlatski, *Onekotorykh voprosakh teorii obshchenarodnogo sotisialistichekogo gosudarstva* (Moscow: SGIP, 1962), focusing on the evolution of socialist society and of the functions of the state in the stage of mature socialism; and D. Chesnokov, *Ot gosudarstvennosti k obshchestvennomu samoupraveniu* (Moscow, 1960), speaking of the development of public organizations to take over the functions of the state—an idea that was launched by Khrushchev.

With regard to the party and state apparat constituting the dominant bureaucracy or ruling group, several authors have advanced the thesis that these were a social class. Milovan Djilas considers the new class to be an ownership class (*The New Class*, London: Allen & Unwin, 1966). Wlodzimierz Brus rejects Djilas's assertion that there has been no socialization of the means of production in socialist countries but only the replacement of one exploiting class by another (the "central political bureaucracy"): "If we accept Djilas' thesis that the aim of this new class is its own material advantage, one would expect that the members of this new class would have an unusually high level of income and that there would be an enormous difference between their incomes and those of other social strata. Taking all elements of income into account, formal and informal, there is no evidence for this" (*The Economics and Politics of Socialism*, London: Routledge & Kegan Paul, 1973).

Much earlier, Bruno Rizzi argued that in Soviet society the bureaucrats in power do not appropriate surplus value directly, like the capitalists, but indirectly by means of the state, which the former control (*La bureaucratisation du monde*, Paris, 1939). Such an assessment is shared by S. Stojanovic of Yugoslavia, who claims that the bureaucracy appears as a collective owner of the means of production; hence a part of surplus value its members appropriate for personal consumption is determined by their status in the state hierarchy ("Etatisticki mit socijalizma," *Praxis*, 1967).

Other authors take the view that the bureaucracy cannot constitute a social class. The Yugoslav Marxist Miroslav Peculic argues that the bureaucracy's control of government is not based on its own property rights but on a delegation of rights: "The bureaucracy does not have its own economic basis founded on personal property and thus it has no historically lasting and stable place in the production process as a class." The quotation is from Branko Horvat, *An Essay on Yugoslav Society* (White Plains, N.Y.: 1969, pp. 77-78), where we find this excellent description of the stratified structure of an etatist society: "The ruling elite which may be called the politocracy is comprised of full time party officials and top bureaucrats (civil and military). Cadres circulate constantly and systematically between technical (bureaucratic) jobs and political (party) positions. In this way the cadres acquire the necessary technical and political experience to rule the society. Nominally, party offices are elective, but actually the organizational bureau or its equivalent make sure the right people are allocated to the right places. The lower echelons of the bureaucracy–that is below the leadership level–represent the etatist service stratum. The rest–the large majority of the population–are the masses: workers and the most inferior stratum, peasants. Forced labor plays the role of the etatist lumpenproletariat.

The (historical) role of the elite–of the vanguard–is to lead; of the masses to be led. This fundamental 'division of labor' is clear, consistent and rigid" (p. 81).

See also pertinent Western books: Merle Fainsod, *How Russia is Ruled*, 2nd ed. (Cambridge, Mass., 1963); Adam B. Ulam, *The Russian Political System* (New York, 1974); Jerry F. Hough, *How the Soviet Union is Governed* (Cambridge, Mass.: Harvard University Press, 1979); Robert Conquest, *Power and Policy in the USSR* (London: Macmillan, 1961); R. A. Bauer, A. Inkeles, and C. Kluckhohn, *How the Soviet System Works* (New York: Vintage Press, 1960).

25. Walter Lippmann, "The Reappraisal," *New York Herald Tribune*, 29 February 1961.

26. Joseph Fitchett, "Europe Acts to Join Era of Innovation," *International Herald Tribune*, 28 November 1985.

27. Joseph Fitchett, "At 28, EC is Still Far From a Common Market," *International Herald Tribune*, 2 December 1985.

28. John Lewis Gaddis, "The Rise, Fall, and Future of Detente," *Foreign Affairs* (Winter 1983-41): 360.

29. Lenin, *Collected Works*, vol. 32 (Moscow: 437).

SELECTED BIBLIOGRAPHY

Bahro, Rudolf. *The Alternative in Eastern Europe*. London: NLB, 1977.

Bergson, Abram, and Herbert S. Levine, eds., *The Soviet Economy Today: Toward the Year 2000*, London: Allen & Unwin, 1983.

Bialer, Seweryn. *The Soviet Paradox*. New York: Random House, 1986.

Brus, Wlodzimierz. *The Economics and Politics of Socialism*. London: Routledge & Kegan Paul, 1973.

Bukharin, Nikolai. *Put'k sotsializmu i raboche-krestianskii soiuz* (The Path to Socialism and the Worker-Peasant Union). Moscow, 1925.

Burlatski, F. M. *O nekotorykh voprosakh teorii obschenarodnogo sotsialisticheskogo gosudarstva* (Some Theoretical Problems on All-People's Socialist State). Moscow: SGIP, 1962.

Carr, E. H. *The Bolshevik Revolution, 1917-1933*. London: Penguin, 1950.

Carrere d'Encausse, Hélene. *L'Empire Eclate*. Paris: Flammarion, 1978.

Chesnokov, P. *Nekotorye aktual'nye voprosy marxisto-leninskoi teorii* (Some Current Problems of Marxist-Leninist Theory). Moscow, 1967.

Chkhikvadze, V. M. *Razvitie narodnoi sushchnosti sotsialisticheskogo gosudarstva* (Development of the Popular Essence of the Socialist State). Moscow: SGIP, 1966.

Cohen, Stephen F. *Bukharin and the Bolshevik Revolution*. New York: Knopf, 1977.

Conquest, Robert. *Power and Policy in the USSR*. London: Macmillan, 1961.

Deutscher, Isaac. Stalin. New York: Vintage Press, 1960.

Djilas, Milovan. *The New Class*. London: Allen & Unwin, 1966.

Fainsod, Merle. *How Russia Is Ruled*. Cambridge: Mass, 1963.

Goldman, Marshall I. *USSR in Crisis: the Failure of an Economic System*. New York: Norton, 1983.

Horvat, Branko. *The Political Economy of Socialism*. New York: Sharpe, 1982.

Hough, Jerry F. *How the Soviet Union is Governed*. Cambridge: Mass. 1979.

Heller, Mikhail, and Aleksander M. Nekrich. *Utopia in Power: The History of the Soviet Union from 1917 to the Present*. New York: Summit Books, 1986.

Kennan, George F. *Russia and the West*. New York: Mentor, 1960.

Lepeskhin, A. T. *Obshchenarodnoe gosudarstvo i ego osnovnyie cherty* (All-People's State and Its Basic Characteristics) Moscow: SGIP, 1961.

Lewin, Moshe. *Political Undercurrents in Soviet Economic Debate: From Bukharin to Modern Reformers*, Princeton, 1974.

Mandel, Ernest. *Marxist Economic Theory*. New York: Monthly Review Press, 1969.

Medvedev, Roy. *Let History Judge: The Origin and Consequences of Stalinism*. New York: Knopf, 1971.

Nove, Alec. *The Soviet Economic System*. London: Allen & Unwin, 1977.

Pipes, Richard. ed. *Revolutionary Russia*. Cambridge, Mass., 1968.

Richta, Radovan. *Civilization at the Crossroads*. White Plains, N.Y.: International Arts and Sciences Press, 1969.

Schapiro, Leonard. *The Communist Party of the Soviet Union*. New York, 1960.

Shakhnazarov, Georgi. *The Role of the Communist Party in Socialist Society*. Moscow: Novosti, 1974.

Shvets, I. A., and I. N. Iudin. *Kak stroitsya, zhivet, deistvuet KPSS* (How The CPSU Is Growing, Living, and Acting). Moscow: Politizdat, 1980.

Stalin, I. V. *Voprosy Leninizma*. Moscow, 1945. *Economic Problems in the USSR*. Moscow, 1951.

Trotsky, Leon. *History of the Russian Revolution*, 3 vols. London: Gollancz, 1932.

Tucker, Robert, ed. *Stalinism*. New York: Norton, 1977.

INDEX

ABOUT THE AUTHOR

SILVIU BRUCAN is professor of social sciences at the University of Bucharest. A participant in the anti-fascist underground movement during the Second World War, he became in 1944 the acting editor of SCINTEIA, the leading daily communist paper of Romania. From 1956 to 1959 he was Romania's ambassador to Washington, and from 1959 to 1962 its ambassador to the United Nations. He subsequently served as the head of Romanian Television and since 1966 has been teaching at the University of Bucharest. Over the last twenty years, he has been lecturing and teaching at universities in the United States and Britain, and at the Sorbonne. Professor Brucan published previously three books in English: *The Dissolution of Power: A Sociology of International Relations* (Knopf, 1971), *The Dialectic of World Politics* (Macmillan, 1978), and *The Post-Brezhnev Era* (Praeger, 1983). He participated in the Tinbergen Report for the Club of Rome, and was Vice-President of the International Studies Association.

www.ingramcontent.com/pod-product-compliance
Ingram Content Group UK Ltd.
Pitfield, Milton Keynes, MK11 3LW, UK
UKHW041121071026
15587UKWH00009B/35

9 780275 927820